P9-ARZ-738

THE HEALING MIRACLES OF
ARCHANGEL
RAPHAEL

ALSO BY DOREEN VIRTUE

BOOKS/KITS/ORACLE BOARD

The Angel Therapy® Handbook (available January 2011)

Angel Words (with Grant Virtue;
available November 2010)

Archangels 101 (available October 2010)

The Art of Raw Living Food (with Jenny Ross)

Signs from Above (with Charles Virtue)

The Miracles of Archangel Michael

Angel Numbers 101

Solomon's Angels (a novel)

My Guardian Angel (with Amy Oscar)

Angel Blessings Candle Kit
(includes booklet, CD, journal, etc.)

Thank You, Angels!
(children's book with Kristina Tracy)

Healing Words from the Angels

How to Hear Your Angels

Realms of the Earth Angels

Fairies 101

Daily Guidance from Your Angels

Divine Magic

How to Give an Angel Card Reading Kit

Angels 101

Angel Guidance Board

Goddesses & Angels

Crystal Therapy (with Judith Lukomski)

Connecting with Your Angels Kit
(includes booklet, CD, journal, etc.)

Angel Medicine

The Crystal Children

Archangels & Ascended Masters

Earth Angels

Messages from Your Angels
Angel Visions II
Eating in the Light (with Becky Prelitz, M.F.T., R.D.)
The Care and Feeding of Indigo Children
Healing with the Fairies
Angel Visions
Divine Prescriptions
Healing with the Angels
"I'd Change My Life If I Had More Time"
Divine Guidance
Chakra Clearing
Angel Therapy®
The Lightworker's Way
Constant Craving A–Z
Constant Craving
The Yo-Yo Diet Syndrome
Losing Your Pounds of Pain

AUDIO/CD PROGRAMS

Angel Therapy® Meditations
Fairies 101 (abridged audio book)
Goddesses & Angels (abridged audio book)
Angel Medicine (available as both 1- and 2-CD sets)
Angels among Us (with Michael Toms)
Messages from Your Angels (abridged audio book)
Past-Life Regression with the Angels
Divine Prescriptions
The Romance Angels
Connecting with Your Angels
Manifesting with the Angels
Karma Releasing
Healing Your Appetite, Healing Your Life
Healing with the Angels
Divine Guidance
Chakra Clearing

DVD Program
How to Give an Angel Card Reading

Oracle Cards
(44 or 45 divination cards and guidebook)

Archangel Raphael Healing Oracle Cards
Archangel Michael Oracle Cards
Angel Therapy® Oracle Cards
Magical Messages from the Fairies Oracle Cards
Ascended Masters Oracle Cards
Daily Guidance from Your Angels Oracle Cards
Saints & Angels Oracle Cards
Magical Unicorns Oracle Cards
Goddess Guidance Oracle Cards
Archangel Oracle Cards
Magical Mermaids and Dolphins Oracle Cards
Messages from Your Angels Oracle Cards
Healing with the Fairies Oracle Cards
Healing with the Angels Oracle Cards

Doreen's beautiful line of Archangel Jewelry is also available via the Hay House Website—keyword: *jewelry.*

All of the above are available at your local bookstore,
or may be ordered by visiting:

Hay House USA: **www.hayhouse.com**®
Hay House Australia: **www.hayhouse.com.au**
Hay House UK: **www.hayhouse.co.uk**
Hay House South Africa: **www.hayhouse.co.za**
Hay House India: **www.hayhouse.co.in**

Doreen's Website: **www.AngelTherapy.com**

THE HEALING MIRACLES OF
ARCHANGEL RAPHAEL

DOREEN VIRTUE

HAY HOUSE, INC.
Carlsbad, California • New York City
London • Sydney • Johannesburg
Vancouver • Hong Kong • New Delhi

Copyright © 2010 by Doreen Virtue

Published and distributed in the United States by: Hay House, Inc.:
www.hayhouse.com • *Published and distributed in Australia by:*
Hay House Australia Pty. Ltd.: www.hayhouse.com.au • *Published
and distributed in the United Kingdom by:* Hay House UK, Ltd.:
www.hayhouse.co.uk • *Published and distributed in the Republic
of South Africa by:* Hay House SA (Pty), Ltd.: www.hayhouse.co.za •
Distributed in Canada by: Raincoast: www.raincoast.com • *Published
in India by:* Hay House Publishers India: www.hayhouse.co.in

Editorial supervision: Jill Kramer • *Project editor:* Alex Freemon
Design: Riann Bender

All rights reserved. No part of this book may be reproduced by
any mechanical, photographic, or electronic process, or in the form
of a phonographic recording; nor may it be stored in a retrieval system, transmitted, or otherwise be copied for public or private use—
other than for "fair use" as brief quotations embodied in articles and
reviews—without prior written permission of the publisher.

The author of this book does not dispense medical advice or
prescribe the use of any technique as a form of treatment for physical,
emotional, or medical problems without the advice of a physician,
either directly or indirectly. The intent of the author is only to offer
information of a general nature to help you in your quest for emotional
and spiritual well-being. In the event you use any of the information
in this book for yourself, which is your constitutional right, the author
and the publisher assume no responsibility for your actions.

Library of Congress Cataloging-in-Publication Data

Virtue, Doreen.
  The healing miracles of Archangel Raphael / Doreen Virtue. -- 1st ed.
    p. cm.
  ISBN 978-1-4019-2472-0 (hardcover : alk. paper) -- ISBN 978-1-4019-
2473-7 (pbk. : alk. paper) 1. Spiritual healing. 2. Miracles. 3. Healing-
-Religious aspects. 4. Raphael (Archangel) I. Title.
  BL65.M4V57 2010
  203'.1--dc22
                                        2009041652

ISBN: 978-1-4019-2472-0

13 12 11 10   4 3 2 1
1st edition, May 2010

Printed in the United States of America

To Archangel Raphael,
with eternal gratitude.

CONTENTS

INTRODUCTION

This is a nondenominational book about the arch-angel named Raphael, a powerful celestial being who heals people and animals. Raphael (pronounced *Raf-ee-el*) is the supreme healer in the angelic realm. In fact, his name means "God heals" or "He who heals" in Hebrew. Many believe that it is derived from the Hebrew word *Rophe,* which means "medicine doctor."

Although Raphael isn't named specifically in the tra-ditional Bible, theologians identify him as the archangel who healed the feeble at the Bethesda pond described in the Gospels. He is also reputed to be one of the three angels who visited the patriarch Abraham and his wife Sarah to announce and help with their children's concep-tion, who healed Abraham's grandson Jacob's wrestling injuries, and who gave King Solomon his magical ring.

In Catholicism, he is Saint Raphael, the patron of healing, physicians, travelers, and matchmakers. Raphael appears by name in the canonical (that is, considered part of the Bible by the Roman Catholic and Eastern

Orthodox churches since A.D. 397) Book of Tobit. This book, sometimes called the Book of Tobias, was lost and later rediscovered as a Dead Sea Scroll in Qumran, the temple of the ancient Essenes, in the 20th century.

The book describes the story of Tobit, a devoted and helpful Jewish man who became so despairing when he went blind that he asked God to let him die. The same evening of Tobit's prayer, a woman named Sarah also begged God for death, out of grief for seven husbands who had each died on her wedding night.

So God answered both Tobit's and Sarah's prayers by sending the archangel Raphael in human form. Raphael didn't identify himself as an angel, but instead offered to protect and guide Tobit's son Tobias as he journeyed to retrieve money that was owed to him.

Raphael led Tobias to Sarah, and the two fell in love and married. The archangel then helped Tobias successfully cast off the demons that had killed Sarah's previous husbands, using fish as part of his healing work. Raphael also used an ointment made from fish to help Tobias heal his father's blindness. As Tobit, Tobias, and Sarah enjoyed their new life, Raphael recovered Tobit's money for him. Once his work was done, Archangel Raphael revealed his true identity and returned to the angelic realm.

The story inspired Raphael to be named a patron saint of physicians, travelers, the blind, and matchmakers. In this book, we'll explore these roles, which he continues to fill.

Raphael's name also appears in another Dead Sea Scroll writing, the Book of Enoch, in which his role upon Earth is described as being "one of the holy angels, who is over the spirits of men." In this text, the Lord charges Raphael with the task of healing the earth of the mess made by some fallen angels and giants—by binding and casting out a demon, helping all of the children, and saving the world from corruption. Archangel Raphael is still focused on this mission today.

Archangel Raphael and You

I frequently get letters from people who are surprised that angels help humanity. They seem astonished or doubtful that famous angels such as Michael, Raphael, and Gabriel would help the average person, especially in modern times. "Aren't these angels from the Bible?" they write to me. Well, yes, *and* they continue to help us thousands of years later.

Angels are God's messengers, sent to Earth to enact the Creator's plan of peace for everyone. To create this experience upon Earth, we need a planet full of peaceful people . . . including you and me. So the angels' mission is to do whatever is necessary to help everyone be at peace. Since health issues can interfere with this feeling, it's natural that God would enlist Archangel Raphael to bring about wellness to people everywhere.

You needn't be special, "chosen," religious, or even a good person in order to receive the angels' healing help. The angels assist everyone, because they love everyone . . . and because it's God's will for everyone to be at peace.

Every person has guardian angels with them at all times. These celestial beings are egoless helpers, guides, and protectors. You also have at least one departed loved one watching over you. While your friends and relatives in Heaven aren't technically angels (since they have human egos), they can still perform angel-like feats. They also work in conjunction with your angels when you're in need.

The term *archangel* (pronounced *ark-an-gel*) is derived from the Greek phrase "the greatest messenger of God." *Arch* means "the first" or "the greatest," and *angel* means "messenger of God."

Archangels are larger, more powerful, and more specialized than guardian angels. Spiritual texts have described dozens of archangels, although most major religions narrow this list to four or seven. Raphael *always* makes the list of top archangels, along with Michael, the protector angel; and Gabriel, the messenger angel.

Since archangels have no egos or physical bodies, they're completely unlimited beings. This means that they can be with countless people simultaneously, having personalized interactions with everyone who calls for help. For this reason, please don't worry that you're bothering the angels by calling upon them.

I must emphasize that we're not worshipping, or praying to, angels. We give all glory to God, Who is the Creator of the angels—and of you and me. However, the angels and archangels are palpable conduits of connecting with the Creator. God created angels as intercessors so that we'd work with them to create peace on Earth.

Sometimes people ask me, "Why should I talk to angels when I can just as easily talk with God?" This is an excellent question, so I prayed about it a long time until I received an answer that brought me peace:

If you can clearly hear the voice of God and feel an unfettered connection to God, then that is Who you should talk to. However, many people become so upset during health crises that they can no longer hear the very high vibration of God's guidance. They must at that point talk with the angels, who are able to match our vibrations no matter how stressed we become.

The angels are God's gifts to us all. And just like any gift, they are meant to be appreciated. God's intention is for the angels to help us.

Seeing Raphael

I've seen angels since I was a very young girl (a spiritual gift that's quite normal among highly sensitive children). So my interactions with Raphael are quite visual and emotional. I see him as a close and trustworthy friend to all. He has a great sense of humor; and like the most brilliant of comedians, his humor is always kind, gentle, and loving. In this way, Raphael reminds us of laughter's powerful curative effects.

Since angels don't have bodies, when a person *does* see them (during crises, dreams, psychic readings, visitations, and so forth), they appear in a form that best helps him or her. I've noticed that the archangels' physical appearance is symbolic of their specialties. For example, Archangel Michael is the epitome of rippling muscles and a toned physique because he's the protector angel. Archangel Raphael, on the other hand, has a more relaxed appearance than Michael, probably because it's *healthy* to be relaxed!

Additionally, the specialty of each archangel creates a surrounding energy field, which visually sensitive people see as colored sparkling light. Archangel Michael's energy looks royal blue and purple, and Archangel Raphael's color is emerald green. Many times when people have asked God to send Archangel Raphael to heal them, they'll begin to see bright green lights with their physical eyes. Noticing green sparkles or flashes of light is one sign that Raphael is with you.

You can also visualize emerald green light around the person or bodily area in need of healing as a way of invoking Archangel Raphael's presence and healing energy.

Raphael is depicted in paintings as the angel guiding Tobias, and he's frequently represented with the caduceus healing symbol (the winged-staff insignia on the cover of this book). And as you'll read in the pages that follow, his healing miracles are vast and varied.

Many people report seeing the name Raphael on license plates, clerks' name tags, and so forth as a way of validating the healing angel's presence. One thing's for sure: Archangel Raphael isn't bashful about letting you know that he's with you, because relaxing into the knowledge of his presence has curative effects.

Feeling Raphael

In addition to seeing signs from Archangel Raphael, many people feel his presence. As you'll read in the stories within this book, the archangel creates palpable physical feelings when he conducts healings. Most people remark on his profoundly gentle energy, which brings great comfort, faith, and trust. Those who have been healed by Raphael also report warm, tingling sensations as they receive his healing energies.

While I was writing this book, I experienced Archangel Raphael's healing power firsthand when I started to develop a bad cold. I asked the archangel to heal me, and within moments, all traces of illness had vanished! In the pages to come, you'll read how Raphael can heal anything from the common cold to serious diseases . . . all you have to do is ask.

CHAPTER ONE

HEALING MIRACLES

*"Dear God and Archangel Raphael, I need a miracle now.
Please heal my body completely and restore me to health.
Please clearly guide my path of wellness, support me in all
ways, and help me feel whole and healthy now."*

Archangel Raphael's chief role is to support, heal, and guide in matters involving health. He uses a variety of methods, including direct intervention, where he miraculously and instantly heals ailments; and guidance, where he directs the person toward the best avenues to health.

After reading and hearing thousands of case studies, I believe that God and Raphael choose the best avenues and methods for healing each particular condition. I also believe that there's a Divine order behind every situation, even if our human minds can't completely comprehend the whys and hows.

Mostly, human free will is the catalyst and the culprit within each health situation. God and the angels can't interfere with our freewill choices. They must wait until we freely ask for help before they can intervene.

How to Ask for Archangel Raphael's Healing Help

So how do you ask for Heaven's help with health concerns? There are unlimited ways to do so, as you'll read within the examples in this book. For example, you can:

- Say your request aloud
- Direct your prayer to God
- Address both God and Archangel Raphael
- Include your preferred religious figure (Jesus, a saint, and so on)
- Think the prayer
- Write the request
- Say the words softly or in a loud voice
- Say the prayer with reverence or with frustration
- Say a supplication prayer, imploring Heaven to address your need (for example, "Please help me!")
- Use an affirmative prayer, affirming that help is already given (for example, "Thank you for helping me")

It's not important *how* you ask for help, but only that you *do* ask for it. Here are important points to remember when requesting Archangel Raphael's assistance:

1. Ask for help, either aloud or silently. He can only help if you ask, because he won't violate your free will.

2. Pour your heart out to Raphael, explaining your feelings.

3. Visualize emerald green healing light surrounding the health concern.

4. Notice and follow any Divine guidance that comes to you in terms of intuitive directions as to which action steps to take.

5. Keep asking for help until healing occurs.

When you ask for help, don't tell God and the angels *how* to go about it. That's called "outlining," and it blocks or slows the answer to your prayers. When you outline, you may overlook the answer because you're focused on other expectations. Let Heaven lead the way with solutions that exceed human imagination and expectations.

In the following stories, you'll read about people who made the choice to ask for Heaven's help with their health. Notice the wide variety within their answered prayers.

Praying for Someone Else

Archangel Raphael responds to all prayers, including those made on behalf of other people. If the ill person accepts his help, the combination of more than one person's prayers is very powerful.

Although the archangel can't impose his help upon an ill individual who doesn't want spiritual assistance, you can request that he be with another person—and his very presence has a healing effect.

Helle Brisson is a certified Angel Therapy Practitioner® who called upon Raphael for a severely ill friend, with miraculous results! Helle recalls:

I have a dear friend who'd suffered from chronic kidney failure and who spent several hours a week hooked up to a dialysis machine. She couldn't go far from home because of the dialysis schedule and because she was signed up for a kidney transplant, for which she had to be available on short notice.

One day after dialysis, she asked me to drive her to a nearby hospital for emergency surgery to reopen the dialysis shunt on her wrist. While she was in surgery, I sat and prayed. I asked Archangel Raphael to heal my friend completely. I then noticed a tapping on my right shoulder. Yet, when I turned around to see who wanted my attention, no one was there! I decided it was a muscle spasm, until the tapping resumed . . . and it finally dawned on me that the angels were signaling me.

So I mentally asked, *Is somebody trying to contact me?*

The answer came instantly through an inner voice: *You're in a hospital. Look around you!* I looked around and all the furniture in the cafeteria was emerald green, the color associated with Arch-angel Raphael! I laughed out loud and thanked him in my head for being there.

You asked for your friend to be healed completely? I heard him ask inside my mind. And he continued: *Are you sure you want her to be healed completely?*

I thought the question was a bit odd, but answered that yes, of course I would want her to be completely healed.

Consider it done was the prompt reply. The tapping stopped, and Raphael was gone.

I didn't think more about the encounter, as the staff called me shortly afterward to tell me that my friend was ready to leave the hospital. Everything went well in surgery. She was still a bit drowsy, and we didn't speak much on the way home in the car. She went straight to bed when we arrived at my house, so I never had a chance that evening to tell her about my encounter with Raphael.

The next morning, I woke up when my friend called me from her bedroom downstairs. I ran down to see her sitting up in bed laughing! "Helle, Archangel Raphael just visited me! He sat on my bed and said he'd spoken with you yesterday and that you'd asked for him to heal me completely."

I told her about my talk with Archangel Raphael the night before, we laughed and hugged each other, and I felt really blessed to have had the help of an archangel. We were very happy the outcome was so positive.

About a year later, a young man approached my friend (who's a professional artist) at her art show and said, "I've heard your story about your chronic kidney failure, and I want to donate one of my kidneys to you!"

Now, the waiting lists can be years long for transplants, and finding a living donor was very unusual! All the medical tests were done, and they were a perfect match. Hardly believing her luck, my friend was excited but also nervous about the surgery. All went well during the transplantation, and both were out of the hospital within days.

I was out of the country during her surgery, but once again felt the tapping on my shoulder and knew there was a new message from Archangel Raphael. This time his message was very short and precise: *Your friend is now completely healed!*

I thanked him and was so happy for her, and then I realized that when I'd prayed a year earlier, it was not only for a healing that day, but a complete healing, which took place one year later when she had her kidney transplant and no longer needed dialysis. My friend got a new life and a new wonderful friend, and she's doing amazingly well with her donated kidney.

Like Helle, you can ask Raphael to help a loved one's health. You don't need to be specially qualified or trained, just sincere in your request. Archangel Raphael helps everyone who asks, unconditionally and immediately.

Here's an example of a prayer to say on behalf of someone else's health:

"Dear God and Archangel Raphael, please help [name of person] *with* [describe health concern]. *Thank you for giving us all faith and hope, and helping us trust that everything is in Divine and perfect order. Thank you for clearly guiding us if we need to take human action steps for this healing."*

For example, after Michael Muth's father received a new hip joint, he went into a convalescent home. Michael noticed a picture on the wall of the archangel Raphael. So Michael asked Raphael to help his father and to heal him very soon. He received an inner message that his father was well protected, and would recover quickly. And so it was. Michael's father could walk again in a very short time and had no more pain.

Calling Upon Raphael for Your Own Health

When you ask Archangel Raphael for a healing, he immediately goes into action on your behalf. As you'll read, his treatment methods are custom-tailored to each person's situation and needs. Sometimes he performs direct intervention; and the person will feel strong tingling sensations, followed by a complete and instant healing. Other times Raphael will guide the person to the appropriate healing professional.

Archangel Raphael always says yes to every prayer, affirmation, visualization, letter, or other forms of calling for his help. Whether someone prays on your behalf or you talk to him yourself, trust that Raphael will help you with your health.

It doesn't matter *how* you pray, as long as you *do* pray, as Suzie O'Neill discovered when her life became so stressful that she broke out in shingles on her face, which affected her eyesight. Susie'seye doctor said that she'd likely lose vision either partially or fully in her left eye.

After the appointment, Suzie came home and was lying on the bed crying, "Archangel Raphael, please don't let me lose vision in my left eye!"

The shingles cleared up, much to Suzie's doctor's amazement, with no damage to her eye. She didn't tell the doctor, but she knew that it was all because she'd called out to Archangel Raphael to help her eye. She hadn't asked the angel to heal the shingles, but this condition cleared up at the same time.

Since Raphael is revered as an angelic eye doctor (because he healed Tobit's blindness in the Book of Tobit), Suzie's story is particularly meaningful.

Suzie's appeal to Raphael was heartfelt and clear, which is the type of prayer that brings fast results . . . since hesitation about receiving help could block or slow a spiritual healing. So, being 100 percent certain that you *want* a healing is a foundation of experiencing one.

Clearing and Releasing

Much of Raphael's angelic healing involves him clearing away toxic energies that are causing the illness. Just like physical toxins, energetic toxins lead to physical maladies.

In this next story, Charlotte Sison experienced Raphael lifting energy that had "hardened" to the point of feeling and appearing like a helmet around her head. I've seen these etheric helmets and shackles creating pain such as the migraine that Charlotte experienced:

> I developed a fever, with a sore throat, bodyaches, pain, a migraine, nausea, and a dry cough. Since I'd never had an illness with this combination of severe symptoms before, I became afraid—especially since the swine-flu scare was happening right then.
>
> As someone who dislikes taking medication, I decided to ask the angels to help me. So, I started breathing deeply and relaxing myself, and called upon Archangel Raphael to heal me.
>
> I didn't feel anything for the first few minutes but the throbbing on the left side of my head. Nevertheless, I pushed on, relaxing and breathing deeply with my eyes closed and calling upon Raphael.
>
> Then the air in my room suddenly changed, becoming warm. I saw a vision in my head of a winged angel ministering to me, calming me, and massaging my head. I felt and saw his hand starting to lift something from the left side of my head. It took a while and was kind of difficult at first, like a metal helmet nailed to my head.
>
> I saw and felt Raphael slowly remove four nails and then lift the helmet away. I realized that this was the migraine, and the metal helmet symbolized it. He took it off and gave it to Archangel Michael (who was right beside him while he was tending to me), who I assume was to take that "thing" to the light.

I then saw Raphael place a small vacuum in my mouth, sucking the phlegm and mucus from my lungs, nose, and throat. He was very gentle. Raphael then reversed the vacuum and sprayed a green toothpaste-like substance inside my chest. He continued doing this until I saw a vision of a sparkling clean set of lungs.

The last thought I remember before drifting off to sleep was: *The migraine seems to have gone away.* When I woke up that afternoon, my headache and fever were completely gone, and my chest was free of its earlier tightness.

I feel that this was really a miracle. Thank you, Archangel Raphael. I now know to ask for help more often.

You can visualize the archangel with an emerald green blowtorch, lifting away bindings similar to Charlotte's helmet. He also removes energy shackles from the body (common around the neck from being in situations where you're controlled by others), which could lead to restricted movement and pain. Ultimately, though, just call upon Raphael, as Charlotte demonstrated. Here's a sample prayer:

"Archangel Raphael, I ask you to come to me now and remove any energy restrictions or blockages so that I may enjoy health and wellness."

A woman named Deborah learned that Raphael could instantly heal a chronic, long-term condition. Deborah was born with kidney obstructions and complications, and she endured many infections and medical tests.

The doctors recommended surgery, but she procrastinated until she was eventually told that unless she had it, the next illness could mean losing the whole kidney. So she had the surgery in 1998 and healed quite quickly, and life went on.

Then in 2006, Deborah became ill again and was terrified of having another operation or of further complications with her kidneys. Although she begged and prayed for healing, her condition worsened, until doctors said she'd need nuclear-imaging tests and an ultrasound. These tests are very expensive, and Deborah was concerned about how to pay for them. This is when the first miracle occurred, as she recalls:

> The day of my test, the hospital called and said that the nuclear-imaging machine was broken. They said that if I would kindly switch to the following morning, they would compensate my trouble by giving me the testing for free. I agreed very quickly and happily!
>
> During the test, I could see a monitor of my kidney functioning. This is where the second miracle occurred. The monitor showed that my right side was working normally and the left side not at all. So I began asking Archangel Raphael to completely heal my kidney. I relaxed and imagined seeing all of the angels sending my left kidney emerald green healing light. I visualized Archangel Raphael actually working on it to repair it completely; and I kept reminding myself that I was perfect, whole, and complete in every way.

After ten or so minutes, the difference in kidney functioning was remarkable, and we could all quite clearly see that both kidneys were working at about the same level. The next day, I came back to see the specialist, who was so amazed that my kidneys' function was nearly perfect.

The doctor first thought she had the wrong images; then she ensured that the machines were working properly, and finally concluded that this was miraculous and she couldn't see why I was getting sick.

Since this miracle in 2006 with Archangel Raphael, Deborah hasn't had a single recurrence of infection and doesn't expect to ever have one again.

Sudden Illnesses Healed

In addition to chronic conditions such as Deborah's, the healing angel can also cure sudden illnesses, such as the food poisoning experienced by a man named Michael when he was in Hong Kong preparing for a vital meeting. Michael had eaten dinner at a nearby restaurant. Something about the meal wasn't right, but he still ate it because he was famished and tired.

Thirty minutes later, Michael suffered severe food-poisoning symptoms. Besides the pain, he didn't have time to be sick because of his important activities the next morning. He was in Hong Kong alone and needed to complete this meeting so that he could return to his home and job in London.

Michael clutched the sweat-soaked sheets, doubled up in pain. Then, suddenly, he remembered Archangel Raphael. With no other option, he surrendered and in that moment felt a presence next to the bed. His eyes were closed, yet he knew there was someone or something there. Michael says, "It felt like I was being embraced in love. And in an instant, the pain stopped, the fever stopped, and I felt at peace."

The next thing morning, Michael felt incredible, as though nothing had happened. The meeting was a success.

Michael says:

This experience confirmed what I'd read: that the angels are real and incredibly powerful. I knew that what had happened was impossible by Earth's standards. This healing encounter increased my faith and encourages me to call for the angels and surrender in all areas.

When Michael talks about "surrender," he means releasing the need to control the situation single-handedly. Surrender is an important component of receiving a spiritual healing, as it's the equivalent of opening the front door to let the housekeepers in so that they can perform their job.

So often I've worked with people who are afraid to surrender for various reasons (distrust of God, a need to be in control, or an unwillingness to receive, for example). This becomes an issue of free will, then, as Heaven can't help someone who doesn't *want* help.

If you believe you may have control issues, then it's a good idea to ask for help with them. A wonderful prayer is:

"Dear God, please help me relax, trust, and have faith in your miraculous ability to restore my health. Please help me get out of the way so that you and the angels can have full access to my mind, body, and spirit in the name of Divine healing. Amen."

Your Free Will Is Key

Be sure that you truly want a healing. Although it sounds illogical, some people unconsciously block them because deep down, they fear wellness. The reasons include: not wanting to lose "secondary-gain elements" associated with illness, such as receiving sympathy or disability payments; feeling undeserving of Heaven's help; and fear of taking responsibility for their health.

As with everything else involved with your well-being, you can ask God and the angels to heal any fears that could possibly block a healing:

"Dear God and Archangel Raphael, I want to want a healing. I now fully open my heart and mind to you, and ask that you release any known or unknown fears about being healthy. I fully desire with my free will to be open to receiving your healing miracles."

Once you're 100 percent willing and ready to receive a healing, all you need to do is ask for help, as Michael Muth (whose father's hip was healed in the story earlier in the chapter) did. In the past, he often had heartburn, which he treated with lots of medication. After learning about Archangel Raphael, Michael asked him to take away the heartburn. Since then, his symptoms occur very rarely, and he hasn't taken any more medication.

The way in which you ask Archangel Raphael for help is less important than the fact that you do so, as I've emphasized. I do find, though, that when someone becomes desperate for help, their prayers are especially powerful, as Lina experienced:

Many years ago I'd fallen ill with an extremely sore throat from a glandular fever. In pain and unable to swallow, eat, or sleep, I spent a week in tears and despair, unable to receive any medical treatment, since the infection wasn't treatable with antibiotics.

So I spent each day in bed in pain. At 3 A.M. on the fifth day of this illness, I awoke; and on my knees, I cried to Archangel Raphael, begging for relief and for his healing, as I could no longer tolerate this unbearable pain.

Then, exhausted, I went to bed, slept like a log, and awoke the next morning totally symptom free! No pain whatsoever, not one visible sign of illness! Oh, what a miracle! I was so grateful to Saint Raphael for his incredible love and healing.

I think that Lina's prayers were immediately answered because she didn't have any fears about receiving Raphael's treatment. She completely desired Heaven's help, so the archangel didn't need to work around freewill fears, which are the equivalent of a locked door preventing him from entering.

You can also pray affirmatively, as Nicole did when she felt a tingling just under her nose, where she sometimes got painful and embarrassing cold sores. She was guided to meditate while asking Raphael to heal her. So she sat in the garden and mentally recited affirmations like *My nose is completely healed* and *I am completely relaxed and healthy.*

After a few minutes, Nicole felt Raphael say, *It is healed.* Sure enough, when she went indoors, the skin under her nose had returned to its normal color, and the tingling had stopped. After an hour, she felt the blocked energy clearing out. Nicole says, "It was a huge relief and a great reminder to ask for assistance and take the time to receive it."

Nicole's affirmations were a powerful way for her to open the door to healing. Spiritually and energetically, such positive statements have an effect identical to that in the previous story of Lina, who also completely opened the door to Raphael because of her extreme desperation. Both Lina and Nicole had no reservations: they wanted a healing, they asked for it, and they received it.

Feeling Heat and Tingling

Those who receive a healing from Archangel Raphael usually feel heat and tingling during the angel's intervention, as Amanda Peart did after hurting her hip during her coaching work for a basketball team. The injury was very painful, making walking incredibly difficult. Amanda wanted to cry whenever she tried to move! Yet duty called, and the next morning she was on the bus taking the team to their basketball game.

Amanda silently called on Archangel Raphael to heal her hip, as the day ahead would be very difficult with so much pain and limited movement. She immediately felt her hands go very cold; then they went really hot and then tingly. Shortly after that, her hip repeated the same cold, hot, tingly sensations.

When she reached her destination two hours later, Amanda carefully got off the bus and was exceedingly pleased to find that her hip was fully recovered!

The tingling heat is undoubtedly the vast energy that Archangel Raphael generates and runs through the people whom he heals. It's like having a giant surge of electricity course through you, in a pleasant and miraculous way.

Sometimes the sensations have a vibrating effect, as Susan White experienced in the following story:

> I'd been bedridden for days, and my whole body ached with a severe flu. I called upon Archangel Raphael to heal me. I gave myself permission to be fully open to the angels' loving healing energies.
>
> After a little while, I noticed that my body was vibrating, and then there were pulling sensations at different points. This went on for some time. It was an amazing and wonderful feeling to go through. I knew Archangel Raphael was there with me, along with some other loving angels.
>
> When I got up the next morning, my aches, pains, fever, and headache had vanished. Instantly I thanked God, Archangel Raphael, and the angels.

I believe that the tingles and vibrations are waves of Raphael's energy pulsating through the body, like healing laser beams. The vibrations undoubtedly push away toxins and open the body's passages for healthy blood and oxygen flow.

Emerald Green Healing Light

For those who can see energy (either as images in the mind's eye or with the physical eyes), Raphael's presence is accompanied by emerald green light. Interestingly, this is the color that is classically associated with the heart chakra and the energy of love. So Raphael literally bathes the body in love to effect his healings.

Some people see Raphael's emerald green light as sparkles, flashes, or waterfalls of color. You can also visualize emerald green light surrounding any bodily area that you'd like to heal, as Jenn Prothero discovered when she asked Raphael to heal her father.

After Jenn's father was diagnosed with bladder cancer, she immediately started working with Raphael on his behalf. During deep meditations, she asked the archangel to surround her dad's bladder with his healing green light, scrubbing away all energies and cancer cells that weren't serving his highest good. She also asked for her dad's health to be restored.

Jenn's father was at a high risk for stroke during surgery and a candidate for complications. So on the day of surgery, she spent the morning meditating and talking with Raphael and other healing angels. She asked them to take care of every detail to ensure her dad's health and recovery.

After surgery, her father was spry and looked healthy. Jenn continued her vigilance, though, and asked the archangel to surround her dad in a tent of healing energy.

The following morning, Jenn's father said to her, "I feel like I could go for my morning walk." He was released the next day. He had no pain, no infections, and very little discomfort. Jenn says, "I know this is the work of Raphael, and I'm grateful!"

When you're praying for someone undergoing surgery, it's a good idea to ask God and Archangel Raphael to guide the doctor's hands during the procedure. Heaven can't violate the doctor's freewill choices, but Raphael's presence in the operating room (thanks to your invitation) definitely has a healing effect, as Heather Vaughn discovered:

> Last year, my father had a sudden and unexpected quadruple bypass, and I called upon Raphael to guide the doctors, heal my father, and give me the strength to deal with the shock of it all. Each day, I sent my father powerful healing intentions and surrounded him with a green light.
>
> The doctor said that the surgery went more easily than expected and he had no question that my father would recover fully. He *has* totally recovered and is a new man today. He's also happier and healthier than I've seen him in a while.

Heather's prayers were powerful because she asked for the doctors to be spiritually guided, as well as making sure her father was surrounded by healing green light. I've learned that it's important to use detailed prayers such as Heather's, because Heaven needs our permission to intervene into anything.

On the other hand, it's not wise to hand God and Raphael a script of how you expect them to behave during the healing (which, as I mentioned, is called "outlining," a method that can block the answers to your prayers because you'll miss seeing the different ways in which they're actually answered).

The key is to ask for all of the healing details to be handled, yet not tell Heaven *how* to create this healing effect. This is something I'll emphasize a few more times in this book since it's such an essential point.

Raphael Can Heal _Anything!_

Another important point is to know that Heaven can heal anything and everything. Beware of mental blocks such as thinking, *Well, this is too big for Heaven to handle;* or the reverse, but energetically identical, thought: *Oh, this is too small to bother Heaven with.*

The angels once told me, "Matter doesn't matter." They explained that material things, such as bodies, are malleable and therefore easy for them to heal. The angels are happy to help, and they heal anything, including nonorganic materials. After all, the angels know that small stressors add up to unhealthful stress.

My mother, Joan Hannan, healed our broken family automobile and washing machine with prayer. I have vivid memories of Mom, hands folded in prayer and eyes closed, with a peaceful expression as she silently asked for these items to be healed because our limited budget didn't allow for repair or replacement of these machines.

So I'm not surprised that Mary Jean George had success with calling upon Archangel Raphael to heal her car. Mary Jean left her job in mid-2008 during the height of the economic recession. Her income was tight while she sought a new job, with no wiggle room for unexpected expenses. That's why she turned to Archangel Raphael when her car malfunctioned.

Mary Jean's driver's-side electric window started making awful noises because the motor began to burn out. A new motor was $700 plus labor, which she couldn't afford. One particularly difficult day after job hunting with no results, Mary Jean banged on the inside of her driver's door and cried out, "Archangel Raphael, I know you can heal anything! Could you please heal this window's motor?"

The motor continued to squeal each time she rolled the window up or down, and Mary Jean felt a little foolish for asking for Raphael's help, but she thanked him anyway. Several days later, though, the squealing stopped! At first she thought it was a fluke and would start making the same noise again, but it remains silent to this day.

Now, every time Mary Jean rolls down her window, she says with gratitude, "Thank you, Archangel Raphael, for answering my prayers."

As Mary Jean's story and others in this book illustrate, healing occurs within Divine timing. Sometimes it takes place instantly, and other times it seems delayed. Perhaps these seeming delays involve the peeling away of our freewill resistance to healing, or perhaps God sees other factors that first need to be addressed before it can occur.

Have faith and trust that God and Raphael hear your prayers. Now that you've asked for help, you've opened the door for their support, guidance, and assistance.

In the next chapter, we'll look at how Heaven can help the millions of people who suffer pain. With Archangel Raphael's aid, it can be successfully reduced and even eliminated.

CHAPTER TWO

PAIN MANAGEMENT AND REDUCTION

*"Dear Archangel Raphael, thank you for helping
my body feel healthy and well in all ways. Thank you
for helping me to feel vitality and peace."*

Statistics show that millions of people suffer from
chronic or transient pain, and that they spend billions
of dollars annually on pain management. In this chapter,
we'll explore how Archangel Raphael spiritually heals
away physical suffering.

In some instances, the discomfort ceases immediately,
and in other cases it gradually subsides. These stories will
impress upon you Raphael's incredible compassion for
those who are in pain. He stands by everyone in need,
helping them feel healthy and well.

Miraculous Pain Prevention

Archangel Raphael can certainly ease and erase pain.
But he can also prevent it from occurring in the first

place. Rose Nickerson's story is miraculous and very touching (grab a tissue before reading it!):

> I was in the hospital, very sick and afraid. I'd collapsed a few days before, and the doctors didn't know what was wrong. All the tests were inconclusive. My arms were bruised and swollen from all of the blood work and injections, since I'm petite, with tiny veins.
>
> It was early morning when a nurse came for another blood draw to see if I was bleeding internally. She was ordered to take 15 vials! And because my arms were in such bad shape, she had to draw the blood from my hand—the most painful place to do it!
>
> I was afraid of needles, and in so much pain that I cried. The nurse said, "I'm so sorry, but we have to do this," and gave me ten minutes to mentally prepare while she gathered her supplies.
>
> I'd brought the book *The Miracles of Archangel Michael* to the hospital with me and remembered reading that Michael and Raphael work together.
>
> So I said repeatedly, "Please, dearest archangels Michael and Raphael, I ask for your help in getting through this as quickly and painlessly as possible. Please be here with me now and negate my fear, anxiety, and pain!"
>
> The nurse came back, told me to lie back, and raised my bed. I closed my eyes and envisioned Raphael's healing green light surrounding me, and I felt Michael on my left side and Raphael on my right, holding my hands.

As the nurse drew the blood, I was astonished that I felt absolutely no pain. I was warm and calm, even serene, as she drew all 15 large test tubes of blood from my hand. It took about 20 full minutes, and I didn't even twinge. I just lay back on my pillow and thanked the beautiful archangels for helping me.

Afterward, I told the nurse about my prayer to the archangels, and she smiled at me and said, "They're always here for us. We just need to ask for their help."

Later that day, it was confirmed that I wasn't bleeding internally and that it was a bacterial infection that was making me so sick. I was treated and was able to go home two days later, with no more tests or needles.

Rose's story illustrates Raphael's remarkable ability to help those in dire need. He makes the seemingly impossible, possible. In desperate situations such as hers, the only thing you can do is pray.

While Silvia's situation wasn't quite as dire as Rose's, she also had no choice but to rely upon Raphael for pain prevention. When her teeth became infected, her dentist recommended extraction. But since Silvia couldn't tolerate anesthesia or sedatives, she had to call upon Raphael. So she told her dentist to pull out her infected teeth without medication. The dentist was against this decision, though, saying she'd experience terrible pain. But Silvia knew that it was the right choice, so the dentist finally agreed.

Two days before the extraction, Silvia focused upon meditation, prayers, and communing with Archangel

Raphael. She asked him to protect her from pain and complications.

The day of her extraction, Silvia told her dentist, "It will be okay. I won't be here; I'll be in the woods." She and the dentist both laughed. As he prepared to extract her teeth, Silvia visualized green energy and light from Archangel Raphael.

After two yanks, the teeth came out. Silvia had no medicine and said she experienced no pain! The dentist was impressed, and told her he didn't understand how that was possible. She explained a bit about meditation, and encouraged him to try it. The wound healed rapidly afterward. Silvia says, "I know now how truly connected I am to Archangel Raphael."

Divine Guidance

Archangel Raphael answers prayers in two ways:

1. Through direct intervention. He heals the situation immediately or gradually, without your further involvement.

2. Through intuitive instructions, which—if you follow them—will lead to the healing you've asked for.

The second method is called "Divine guidance," meaning that Raphael whispers instructions in your inner ear or thoughts, or sends you a message in your mind's eye or through intuitive feelings. Raphael guides you to take purposeful steps that result in healing.

You can recognize Divine guidance because it's repetitive. You'll have a continual urge to take certain actions, and you may not realize why you have this idea. But if you trace it back in time to its origination, you'll find that it occurred right after you prayed for a healing.

Those who follow their Divine guidance are always rewarded, and those who distrust and ignore it complain that God isn't answering their prayers. Yet when we disregard Divine guidance, it's we humans who are ignoring Heaven's outstretched hand.

Lisa Smith is very glad that she followed her Divine guidance, which came in the form of an inner voice. Since adolescence, she had suffered extreme abdominal pain during her monthly cycle. So she'd pop the highest-dose pain-relief pill she could, four at a time every two hours, because she was in such agony.

Doctors told her to take birth-control pills, but they didn't help. Then she was rushed to the hospital with a burst fallopian tube that had been blocked, and incidentally, was causing the pain. After a big operation and 11 weeks to recoup, Lisa anticipated a pain-free life. But to her horror, the pain returned, worse than ever, and doctors to this day don't know why.

Fortunately, Lisa discovered the angels through spiritual books and classes. One night she called upon Archangel Raphael and, to her amazement, she felt a presence of pure love and warmth. Then she saw the color green clearly and powerfully. Lisa asked Raphael to heal her of these horrible pains.

Lisa recalls:

> I heard an inner voice instruct me to soak in
> a warm bath, then place my hands on my lower

abdomen and "call upon Raphael" two days prior to my menstrual period. I wasn't sure if I'd made the whole experience up or not, but I figured, *What do I have to lose by trying?*

So, two days prior to her period, she followed the instructions exactly. As before, she felt the warmth and could see green, but this time it was like someone else's hands were upon her. The heat was also very powerful!

Although Lisa had doubted whether this would work, to her pleasant surprise she never had any more pain, and never had to take another pill!

Lisa says:

> This was a miracle! I still let my ego tell me that it was coincidental. All I can say is that ever since that day, I've done the same healing monthly, and the pain has never returned. I don't even buy painkillers anymore. Archangel Raphael saved me from hiding every month and living in fear of suffering! Raphael is the modern woman's healing angel!

If you receive intuitive guidance and you're unsure if it's real Divine guidance, you can always ask the angels to give you clear signs as to its validity. Here are some key characteristics that help you distinguish true from false guidance:

1. True guidance comes in response to prayer. False guidance comes in response to worry.

2. True guidance is consistent and repetitive. False guidance changes its mind constantly.

3. True guidance is to the point. False guidance meanders.

4. True guidance focuses upon action. False guidance focuses upon "What's in it for me?" (is egocentric).

5. True guidance feels warm and safe. False guidance feels cold and sneaky.

A woman named Tawn Head decided to try following her Divine guidance, with spectacular results:

> I was listening to an old episode of the *Angel Therapy* show on the Hay House Radio® archives. A caller was having pain, and Doreen walked her through asking Raphael to do his healing work.
>
> So I asked Raphael what I could do to alleviate the pain in my feet. I heard in my head, or rather, had a knowing in my mind: *Detox by bathing.* I didn't know what to think of this message, since I shower every morning and bathe in saltwater at night. What did he mean? I asked once more, and I got the same answer yet again: *Detox by bathing.*
>
> *Hmm,* I thought. I just didn't understand. Was I to bathe more than one time a day? How would that help me with foot pain? I tried to understand the information as the next couple of hours went by.
>
> Then I thought of my friend Catherine's new business. I remembered that she offered "ion footbaths" at her holistic-healing center, so I

booked a session with her. When I got to the center, I noticed a tall painting. I asked my friend, "Catherine, who is the person in this portrait?"

She answered, "Why, Tawn, that's Archangel Raphael." So I knew I was on the right track! I now do ion footbaths in my own home, and continue to work with Archangel Raphael and the other angels in new and wonderful ways.

With Divine guidance, we work in partnership with God and the angels. Each situation and person is treated individually and uniquely, so do pay attention to repetitive feelings or ideas that occur after you pray for healing help. As with Tawn's story above, you may feel like you're playing detective as you unravel the clues that Raphael gives to you. You'll be glad that you made the effort and followed your guidance, as Hilda Blair discovered.

Hilda had experienced back pain for seven years. Treatments with two chiropractors, work with two acupuncturists, and physical therapy only increased her suffering. Then she learned about Archangel Raphael, whom she immediately asked to take away her back pain.

Instantly, Hilda received inner guidance to stop any exercise or physical therapy. Then she was instructed to stretch in her bed before going to sleep. She was also instructed to visualize herself dancing and experiencing no discomfort. Hilda followed this guidance, and within a month, she had no more pain and continues to be pain free today.

Hilda says she learned that . . .

. . . angels sometimes help us by whispering in our ears and telling us what to do to help ourselves. Now I know my angels lead me to what I need to do through an inner knowing or guidance. Sometimes we do need a doctor's help, but I also know we have Archangel Raphael's when we need it.

Sometimes Archangel Raphael functions as a heavenly physical therapist, guiding people in pain to flex their muscles. When a former nurse named Karen Forrest sprained her back while shoveling snow from her driveway, she immediately called upon Raphael. Karen could barely walk as she appealed to the healing angel for help.

As she invoked Archangel Raphael, Karen immediately felt his comforting presence. She felt heat and tingling sensations surrounding her back. She even visualized green rays of healing light around her back and body. She felt relieved knowing Raphael would help her heal naturally.

Karen silently asked the archangel to let her know what she needed to do in her healing process. That day and the next one, she was guided to lie down four times a day for about 20 minutes to receive continued healing and to allow her body the chance to recover.

Admittedly, this was easy enough the first day, as she wasn't in any condition to move around much. But the second day she was feeling much better, yet still intuitively knew that she needed to rest for her angelic-healing sessions. This wasn't easy to honor, since she's a busy person who doesn't do well lying around. She'd rather ignore any slight back discomfort and continue working.

But Karen had the inner urging to lie down for a bit—and she listened to it.

Karen almost forwent her fourth healing session on the second day, as she was caught up in her administration work. But then she clearly heard: "Go lie down." She knew what these words meant, so she immediately stopped working and lay down for her final angelic-healing session. As with the previous sessions, she felt Archangel Raphael's soothing presence, along with the physical warmth and tingling on her back. She also loved seeing the beautiful green rays of healing light surrounding her.

Karen says, "By the third day, I was back to normal. I know from my nursing background that medically it usually takes about one week to heal from the strain I endured. I was extremely grateful for my amazing angelic healing."

Trust Archangel Raphael to know exactly how to heal your condition. Again, if you're unsure whether your guidance is correct, ask him to repeat, clarify, or verify his message. Don't worry about offending Raphael with impertinence or ingratitude: he's completely focused upon restoring your peace of mind through health.

Sometimes Raphael's Divine guidance consists of "homework" designed to boost your faith in healing. As I've discussed, Heaven can't violate your free will. So if a part of you resists a healing, Raphael may help you open the door to freely accepting his miraculous energies.

Lina needed such help, and Raphael guided her to light candles as focal points so that she could clearly reach the point of wanting a healing and knowing that she deserved Heaven's help. She'd suffered from muscular neck and head tension for eight years and had been controlling the pain with chiropractic assistance. But in 2007 the pain worsened, causing her whole body to go into cramplike spasms that would last for a week. It was very uncomfortable and rendered her not functional. Even worse, no medication was helpful, and test results showed there was no underlying cause.

That's why Lina decided to call upon Archangel Raphael for help. During the week of Easter 2008, she was guided to light six white candles for six straight days. She visualized Raphael's healing green light around her body and thanked him for his love, healing, and protection. Since then, she hasn't experienced any muscular tension!

The candles boosted Lina's clarity, focus, and faith. So, too, did her meditations in which she visualized green light around her body, which is a way of invoking Raphael's healing presence. Additionally, Lina used "affirmative prayers"—thanking Heaven for its help before it appears. This is an effective way to increase faith, because affirmations help you believe in miracles, and faith opens the doorway to healing.

Sometimes Raphael guides people to the appropriate healer. When this occurs, it's up to us to follow his lead and trail of clues, because the person may have skills or tools that release blocks to wellness. Raphael guides people to both traditional- and alternative-medicine healers.

Carmen was guided to one of the graduates of my Angel Therapy Practitioner certification program, and received a profound healing as a result:

> I had chronic pains in my right hip and foot, which my chiropractor attributed to walking

barefoot on tiled floors. Arch supports in my shoes brought some relief, until I gained weight and the pain returned after my second pregnancy.

Although I lost the extra weight and kept using arch supports, the pain continued. One day, I read an article by a local Angel Therapist, so I contacted her for a session. She passed her hand over my leg and foot during the session, while thanking Archangel Raphael for his healing. My pain subsided right away, and months later I no longer have any in my foot and only a slight tingle in my hip. I completely believe that Archangel Raphael has cured this, and I am grateful every day for this healing.

I'm happy to hear that Carmen gave all credit to Archangel Raphael. Even though the practitioner brought his energy through, it was ultimately Heaven that healed Carmen. This is something that I emphasize in my classes so that practitioners don't go into their egos in the face of healing successes. Always, all glory goes to God. We only take credit for being good listeners and open conduits of Divine healing energy.

Divine guidance isn't always profound or exotic. A lot of times it involves commonsense advice, which leads to the reduction or cessation of pain, as a healer named Gillian Smalley discovered when at age 42 she decided to run marathons.

At first, Gillian trained for her races by alternating walking and running until she could gradually run ten kilometers (about six miles). During one race, though, the pain in her right shin was immense. Gillian didn't want to stop, so she slowed down and asked Archangel Raphael to please help take the pain away. When she got the message to walk, she argued that she was just starting to *run* really well.

Gillian got the message to walk again for the next two songs on her iPod. True Divine guidance, after all, is repetitive! So Gillian did as she was told, and after the second song, she started running again. Happily, Gillian finished running the ten kilometers. Now if she ever has pain while running, she asks Archangel Raphael to help immediately. With Raphael's help, she has managed to run seven fun races, all pain free!

Raphael functioned like a running coach for Gillian. I had a similar experience when doing a 6.2-kilometer triathalon recently. When my quadriceps started burning, I asked Archangel Raphael for help, and I ran the rest of the race comfortably and effortlessly.

Instant Miraculous Healing

So as we've just reviewed, sometimes Archangel Raphael heals by giving Divine guidance in the form of intuitive assignments and instructions. Yet other times, he goes directly to people's bodies and instantly heals their pain. Why doesn't he just heal *everyone* instantly? I can only fathom that when Raphael gives guidance, it's a part of that person's spiritual growth or life purpose to learn about self-care and spiritual healing.

Yet, instant healings also create spiritual growth because they boost faith and confidence in Heaven's protective power, as Sandi Mallam discovered after tests following a cerebral hemorrhage revealed a brain tumor.

While hospitalized, Sandi developed migraine headaches, which the doctors said was from the hemorrhage.

When Sandi was discharged from the hospital, she was prescribed pain medication, and for the next two years, she was treated at a pain clinic. Although her medication was changed five times and she also tried acupuncture, the pain continued. The doctors said she'd have to live with it.

But Sandi didn't want to live with the pain, so she asked Archangel Raphael to heal her. She went outside for some fresh air, thinking that it might help a little, and after about 15 minutes she noticed that she felt different but couldn't figure out why. Then she realized: her migraine had vanished!

Sandi rushed indoors to tell her husband that after having the constant pain in her head for years, it was suddenly gone!

Sandi says, "To be pain free after all that time was worth far more to me than winning a lottery. I give thanks to Raphael every day for listening to my prayers that Saturday morning, and now angels are a big part of my life."

I love stories of how Raphael instantly cures long-term conditions, like Sandi's. Imagine how free she must feel, after living under crushing agony for so many years. The angels hold the key to a pain-free life, but we must first give them permission *and* fully open the door for their healing work.

Raphael probably guided Lukas Tobler to read about the archangel's healing work, because once Lukas discovered and called upon him, the healing angel was able to help. In that instant, Lukas's long-term condition immediately vanished.

As a teenager, Lukas had surgery on his right wrist to remove a painful ganglion. The surgery went fine except for a decreased range of motion.

Years later, Lukas was new to working with angels, and he called upon Archangel Raphael to heal his wrist. He was astounded to experience instantaneous relief of the limitation on his range of motion in his right wrist!

Lukas says, "Filled with awe and gratitude, I kept moving my wrist with its newly gained joint mobility. Even years later, I can bend my wrist with complete range of motion."

In addition to chronic issues, Raphael also instantly heals recent injuries. Candace Pruitt-Heckstall experienced pain during a yoga class and received Raphael's immediate help. Among yoga's many benefits is its ability to increase our psychic awareness. Candace psychically saw Raphael's healing treatment in her mind's eye:

My husband and I were doing an intense yoga practice involving stretching and breathing for extended periods of time. If the poses aren't done correctly, it's easy to pull muscles. We had transitioned into a particular pose where our right arms were stretched skyward when I felt my right shoulder seize up in pain. I'd injured that shoulder previously, and this time was quite painful. I mentally called out: *Raphael, please help!*

Suddenly, I saw a clear vision of a person with a large needle and emerald thread stitching my shoulder. Then I saw someone take a small, handheld vacuum and suction the pain away! I knew it was Archangel Raphael helping heal me from my pain, and he did!

Gradual Healing

Sometimes Raphael's healings take longer. After reviewing hundreds of stories, I've concluded that it's advantageous to keep praying for help until it occurs. Repetitive prayers help condition the mind to accept assistance. In other words, they're catalysts that open the door to Raphael's healing. And in that moment when you're ready to accept his help, it will happen, as Anne-Marie Saunders experienced.

When Anne-Marie was pregnant, she suffered a separated pelvis that never healed and that caused her daily pain. She received steroid injections for pain management, but the discomfort worsened. Anne-Marie hurt no matter whether she was standing, sitting, or lying down. The doctor said that surgery was the only option, but at the risk of her pelvic plate snapping.

In desperation, Anne-Marie called upon Raphael to heal her so that she could avoid surgery. Almost immediately, she felt the energy in the room change, as if every cell in her body "stopped" for a split second. She experienced a strange sensation around her pelvic joint, like millions of tiny spiders spinning a web across it—that's the only way she could describe it. This continued for some time, and she eventually fell asleep.

The next day, the pain was reduced. She continued to call upon Raphael nightly when she went to bed. Sometimes her pelvis got very hot, and other times there was a sharp pain and she had to ask Raphael to slow down. Every night for about two months, Anne-Marie invoked Raphael to ask for healing, and every day that followed was a little easier.

After two weeks, she was able to drive short distances again. After about six weeks, she stopped using her walking stick. It's now been three months, and she's much better and has many pain-free days.

Patience and daily prayers healed Anne-Marie, just like following Divine guidance helped the other people in this chapter's stories. In the following chapter, you'll read more about how Raphael heals by sending people to the appropriate physician. The key is to ask for help without expectations of how your healing will occur. Know that every healing prayer is heard and answered, and that *your* answer will be custom-tailored especially for you!

CHAPTER THREE

RAPHAEL
HELPING HEALERS

"Dear Archangel Raphael, thank you for guiding me to the best healer for my health needs and Divine life purpose. Thank you for opening the way for me to receive the best health treatment possible. Thank you for supporting me in all ways as I completely heal now."

Raphael's focus is upon people's health. He's a tireless healer, with an unlimited bag of healing techniques. The archangel also supports those who *are* healers, or those who want to become professional healers.

If you're a current or a would-be healer, you can rest easy knowing that Raphael is guiding your career (provided you ask for his help and then follow any guidance he gives to you). Raphael functions as both a healer's and a patient's advocate by matching up sick people with the best health-care providers.

Raphael's Physician-Referral Service

As if it's not stressful enough to get sick, you also have the daunting task of selecting and paying for the best physician. When you're stressed about an illness, it's difficult to think clearly in picking a doctor. Fortunately, Archangel Raphael can lead you to the appropriate treatment, if you'll ask for his help, as Denise did.

Denise's husband was diagnosed with a serious precancerous condition of the esophagus. Doctors said the only course of action was for him to undergo surgery to remove most of his esophagus. This was a dangerous procedure, and it needed to be performed by a surgeon who did this type of operation routinely.

Their doctor recommended the surgery be done in nearby Boston, at one of the many outstanding medical facilities there. But he gave no specific recommendations, and Denise and her husband were on their own, frightened and unsure about which hospital or surgeon to choose. They only had their doctor's instructions to "find someone as familiar with this surgery as he is with brushing his own teeth."

So Denise asked God and Archangel Raphael for help and guidance as she began researching on the Internet to look for Boston hospitals and doctors specializing in this procedure. Imagine her confusion when several doctors at different hospitals showed up in her online search. She had no idea which way to turn as she scrolled through the names. So she continued asking the archangel for guidance.

Suddenly, one of the doctors listed stuck out because his first name was Raphael. As soon as Denise saw this, she knew that he was the answer to her prayers. She clicked on the link for him and discovered which hospital he worked at in Boston, and all of his information. There was even an e-mail address to contact him directly with questions! She hesitantly wrote him a message explaining the situation. The doctor wrote back within a few hours and wanted all her husband's information, and he set up an appointment to see him almost immediately.

They went to see the doctor, and discovered he was a pioneer in this surgery and one of the best in the country to perform it. People came to him from all over for this procedure. His services were also covered by their medical insurance, which was a miracle in itself.

But the story doesn't end there. As the day of surgery approached, their apprehension grew, and fear set in. After all, this was a risky operation. Their fears were high the day before surgery when Denise and her husband got in the car and headed to Boston. They hadn't been driving very long when Denise's fear reached the point of complete panic, and she was nearly immobilized.

She called out for Archangel Raphael's help in her mind and heart, and asked him for a sign that the surgery would go well. No sooner had she done so than a car pulled out from a side road in front of them. To Denise's utter disbelief and sheer joy, the license plate on the car was a vanity plate that said: "RAPHAEL."

Denise knew in that exact moment that no matter what came next, they'd be okay. She was certain that Archangel Raphael was with them and that they'd picked the right doctor. Denise was immediately filled with an overwhelming sense of calm and peace, and tears of gratitude rolled down her face.

Seven years later, her husband is doing amazingly well and is still having annual visits with the remarkable doctor Archangel Raphael sent them to.

Denise noticed and trusted the signs from above, which led her to Raphael's hand-selected physician. This requires faith, admittedly, because someone could decide that such signs were coincidental. The angels can only do so much when conveying guidance to us. We can meet them halfway there by keeping an open mind and following the clues they give us.

Not only can Raphael guide you to the right physician, but he can also get you an appointment in the doctor's otherwise-full schedule, as Amber discovered. Last year, she noticed that her one-year-old son had an enlarged lymph node. So, she called his pediatrician's office, only to learn there were no appointments available and she needed to go to the walk-in clinic.

But she didn't like the idea of taking a problem like this to a walk-in clinic, and her gut kept telling her to go to the pediatrician's office anyway. On the way there, Amber asked Archangel Raphael to help her son heal and get the kind of treatment he needed.

When she arrived at the pediatrician's office, Amber asked for the doctor to see her son, and they said yes. After the exam, the doctor suggested a specialist who was wonderful with her son and was the top person in his field.

It turned out that Amber's son had a staph infection that had isolated itself in that one lymph node, instead of spreading throughout the body. The doctor was able to drain the fluid from the node. With a series of antibiotics, the infection cleared up, and they were able to leave the hospital. Amber believes that if she hadn't followed the messages Archangel Raphael had sent, her son would have gotten a lot sicker.

Amber says, "Thanks to Archangel Raphael for leading me to the right doctors. I believe he helped stop the infection from spreading and guided the doctors to perform the right treatment. I'm very grateful for all of his help."

Raphael's physician referrals help patients, and also ensure that qualified healers have thriving and successful practices. Raphael knows which healers have pure intentions, talent, and top-notch skills; and the archangel is happy to refer plenty of patients to them.

In addition to medical doctors, Raphael refers clients to practitioners of virtually every healing modality.

Nurses Who Heal with Archangel Raphael

Dedicated nurses truly are Earth angels. They give a lot of themselves, often for long hours and with little recognition. With hospital-staff cutbacks, many nurses are doing the jobs of several people and may even endanger their own health in the process. That's why it's doubly important for them to acquaint themselves with Archangel Raphael's healing support. Not only do nurses benefit from Raphael's presence and guidance, but the patients also receive the archangel's remarkable assistance.

Theresa Dettinger, a registered nurse (RN) who practices energy healing, says that every time she conducts a healing session, she sees and feels Archangel Raphael standing behind her.

Theresa explains:

I can see and feel Raphael enfolding me with his arms and wings. He pours healing energy into and through me. In my mind's eye, this energy is the most brilliant emerald green light, very much like the way the Emerald City glowed in the movie *The Wizard of Oz*. I see this glow emanate from my hands and into my client's body. It's the most warm and comforting sensation, and I'm very grateful to Raphael for his love and assistance.

Another RN named Karen Bishop credits Archangel Raphael with guiding her nursing practice over the past 25 years. In the intensive care unit where Karen works, she calls upon Raphael when she can't locate a vein or get a response from a patient, or the monitor equipment goes haywire. He also helps her deal with devastated family members as she explains their loved ones' medical conditions, as well as in tense interactions with other medical personnel.

Karen says, "Without fail, Raphael helped me with every one of these situations. Everyone should know about Archangel Raphael, who has always come through when asked. I couldn't have been the nurse I was without his assistance."

And RN Carmen Carignan views Archangel Raphael as part of her health-care team. Carmen completely trusts and relies on the guidance she receives from him. She says, "I'll hear his loving, gentle, yet firm guidance. If I ignore him, his guidance becomes louder, almost like a nagging within me, until I listen and follow."

Carmen recalls an incident when a young pregnant woman was admitted to her hospital, in obvious distress. She complained of severe pain along one side of her back, as well as vomiting.

Since the woman was dehydrated, Carmen tried starting her IV, but was unsuccessful in finding a vein. Another nurse also couldn't find one after two attempts.

Carmen says:

> It was then that I called upon Archangel Raphael to assist me in this situation. Almost immediately, I had a knowing of where to go to insert the IV. I asked the patient if she believed in angels. Her response was an immediate "Yes!" I explained to her that I was receiving guidance from Archangel Raphael.
>
> When I proceeded, I couldn't see or feel the vein, yet it was like someone else was guiding my hands. I trusted and went with it. It ended up being one of the easiest and most painless IV sticks I'd ever done. The young woman and I were both amazed by, and grateful for, the outcome.

M.D.'s and Ph.D.'s Working with Raphael

It's a new world in so many ways! I grew up in a family who used spiritual methods (such as prayer, visualization, and affirmations) to heal our bodies, emotions, finances, and relationships (and, as I mentioned in Chapter 1, even our automobile and washing machine!). Yet our methods were considered odd by those who knew about them. So we didn't talk about our prayer work, except with our friends at church.

Today, spiritual healing is not only out of the closet, but it's also openly taught and studied! To me this is a miracle. Only a short time ago, the mind-body medical connection was still a distrusted concept. In fact, when I was pregnant with my son Charles in 1978, my doctor rolled his eyes and smiled when I complained that stress was affecting the pregnancy. He didn't see the connection between stress and physical health. Today, doctors routinely interview their patients about stressors related to their presenting illnesses.

I regularly meet healing professionals at my angel workshops who come from mainstream medical facilities. What impresses me most is their open-mindedness. They care deeply about unlocking healing secrets, because they care about their patients' health . . . even if that means using alternative modalities.

The number of controlled studies of prayer's efficacy for healing grows annually, and their results are impressive! Scientists long ago ruled out the placebo effect as the basis for prayer's healing effect (having confirmed that prayer heals plants, animals, and infants).

Most people I survey say that they'd prefer to have a physician who prays on their behalf. So it's heartening to see spirituality taught in medical classrooms, and practitioners such as Sanja Perko, M.D., bring spirituality into their healing practices.

Dr. Perko first encountered Archangel Raphael during a guided meditation in a small group. As the person leading the meditation introduced everyone to Raphael, Dr. Perko felt a pleasant warmth and a tingling sensation. Then she saw beautiful green and silvery pillars of light that pushed her head up and backward. She had the feeling of floating in the air, as if she were out of body.

Dr. Perko recalls:

> Suddenly, a clear thought came to me: *You are a healer. Raphael will help.* At first I was very surprised, and afterward I spent some time thinking about this experience. I felt that my whole life was a great puzzle, and this wonderful thought was the last piece in the picture.

Through Raphael's presence and message, it became clear to Dr. Perko why she couldn't find a job as a doctor after she finished medical school, why she couldn't work eight hours in the office every day like her father and sister, why she was so interested in herbal medicine and aromatherapy, and why she always had the feeling that there was something more to find and learn.

Dr. Perko says:

> I'm very grateful to Archangel Raphael for his guidance and help. Every morning from that day on, I've thanked my angels for their love and protection. When my children are ill, I treat them with herbal remedies and essential oils, and of course, I always ask Raphael to help and to heal them. And he always does.

For Dr. Perko, the experience of working with Raphael awakened her knowledge and respect for the archangel's healing power. In the same way, the following story shows how the palpable sensations of energy that Raphael emanates led another healing professional to believe.

Diego E. Berman, Ph.D., works at the prestigious Columbia University Medical Center, and openly admits his interest in researching alternative healing methods. To Dr. Berman, it's part of a scientist's job to research every aspect of healing in case there's something that would help patients. Dr. Berman explains: "As a scientist interested in improving people's quality of life, I research healing methods at the physical, emotional, and spiritual levels."

Yet even though he's open-minded, his credulity was tested when a friend offered to do an "angel reading" for him. The concept of talking to angels exceeded his structured scientific mind's belief system.

"However," he recalls, "the very first moment my friend did the angel reading, everything changed within me. I could feel the angelic energy around us. I was amazed; it was such an uplifting experience, and something inside of me had been touched by these angelic beings."

The angel reading opened a spiritual gateway for Dr. Berman. He'd connected with the angels! The following week when he was conducting a healing session, he heard a deep, soothing male voice guiding him to send energy to a different part of the person's body.

Dr. Berman recalls:

As I was trying to make sense of that voice with my intellectual mind, I could see a cloud of a colorful, strong energy floating toward me from the left side of my visual field. I then heard the words *I am Raphael, and I am here to assist you and improve your healing skills.*

As these words were said, a thin thread of energy extended from that cloud and fused with my energy field around my hands. I could feel that the energy I was sending had been intensified.

Raphael then guided me as to how to perform the healing, and he has been with me on every healing session since then. His presence is extremely comforting, reassuring, and professional. I call upon him for advice on all healing situations, and he's always available to suggest the best ways to improve the healing process.

Aren't you grateful that we live in a day and age when doctors and Ph.D.'s allow themselves to believe in angels and spiritual healing, and then openly admit these beliefs? Of course, Archangel Raphael has a way of turning skeptics into believers, as Johanna Vandenberg, Ph.D., discovered.

Dr. Vandenberg holds a doctorate in geriatric studies, and she practices as an Angel Therapist®. She recalls working with a skeptic who became convinced of Archangel Raphael's reality when he saw the angel's signature green light:

A man was in my New York City office for a spiritual-counseling session. I began with my usual question: "What can I do for you?"

He folded his arms and loudly replied, "You tell me!" while staring at me angrily.

So I sighed and silently asked, *Archangel Raphael, please help me with this person.* Suddenly, the man jumped and then sat straight up in his chair with his eyes opened wide. I jumped, too, since he'd startled me.

When I asked him what was the matter, he

slowly said, "There's a green light between us, in front of you!" So I reassured him that this was a sign that Archangel Raphael had come to help us.

He didn't say anything, so I asked him if he was okay. "It's still there," he replied. By the time he left the session, his anger and defensiveness were gone. He came back for several sessions to learn about the angels and fairies. Today, he's a happy, healthy, thriving man who teaches other people about angels, especially Archangel Raphael!

Dr. Vandenberg also works with Raphael for her own family and friends in need. When her godson's father had an asthma attack and had been on a respirator for almost a week, she went to the hospital to see him. His face was very gray, and he was barely conscious.

So Dr. Vandenberg sat next to him and called upon Archangel Raphael for help. Telepathically, she said to the man, *I'll ask the angels to help you, but first I have to ask whether you want to live,* because it was her understanding that she shouldn't force people to stay here if they wanted to leave.

She didn't hear anything for a while, as he was in a deep sleep. But then she heard a faint voice, and telepathically he whispered, *Yes.*

She then asked Raphael to clear the room of negative energies. With the healing angel's help, Dr. Vandenberg sent energy and light to wherever she was guided to relieve the man's congestion.

She recalls:

Several hours later his wife called to say that after I left, his face returned gradually to a pink color, and that night he was taken off the respirator!

This occurred in 2006, and to this day, he's a strong and healthy father who's raising several children and has become a homeopathic doctor! He doesn't remember anything, and his wife thanked me so much, but I was very careful to give all the credit to Raphael and the angels.

Other Healers Who Work with Raphael

Many psychotherapists have taken my Angel Therapy® classes since 1995, when I first began teaching about angels. Most therapists are open-minded and openhearted healers who are sensitive to emotional and physical feelings. They can sense the angels' presence and intuitive messages, perhaps because they've been trained to tune in to their patients' feelings.

I've also worked with a number of psychotherapists who blend traditional and alternative approaches to mental health, for everyone's benefit. Healers who work closely with angels, such as psychotherapist Kristy M. Ayala, find that Heaven guides their healing practice in all ways.

When Kristy tired of the traditional psychology field, she decided that she was ready for a new line of work, even though she was unsure about what that would be. So she devoted time to prayer and meditation, until she was guided to work as a spiritual counselor and healer. Kristy wanted to pursue this career; however, she wasn't certain how to move forward and begin serving clients in this new way.

So Kristy asked Archangel Raphael for guidance and the resources to pursue this work full-time. She asked for support in getting additional training she'd need, and help to move onto this path smoothly.

Kristy says:

> Archangel Raphael consistently intervened to bring the right people, financial resources, and opportunities for me to expand my training. He also provided the emotional, spiritual, and physical support that I asked for. In addition, Archangel Raphael performed healings on me so that I could release issues and blocks that were no longer serving me, which then allowed me to move forward on this path more easily.
>
> Archangel Raphael has also brought clients who are a perfect match to me, and has worked with me to provide them with counseling and healing. He has been a true gift to me from God, allowing me to foster my gifts so that I can complete my Divine life's work in this lifetime.

Those who conduct bodywork and physical therapy frequently mention having interactions with their clients' guardian angels. These health-care professionals remind me of pilots and astronauts who are unsure if they can openly discuss the UFO's they've witnessed. Yet, when you touch someone's body, you are tapping into their energy field—which instruments such as CAT scans scientifically measure. So is it any wonder that bodyworkers also connect with the energy of angels standing next to their clients, as happened to a healer named Mary?

Mary was sitting next to a client who lay on her massage table. Her hands were on each side of her client's temples when suddenly in her right ear she heard a huge booming voice say, *"Raphael!"* Then she heard it *again.*

Mary wasn't afraid . . . just startled by the voice. She immediately felt the energy of this angel throughout her body and throughout the room. Needless to say, the treatment was a very powerful and emotional one.

After the session, Mary got up the nerve to tell her client what had happened. She hoped that the woman was open-minded and wouldn't think she was crazy. When Mary told her, the client sat frozen, pale, and expressionless. Mary's heart sank, and she feared her client was going to bolt out of the room, never to be seen again.

Instead, the woman said in a quiet voice, "He came because I asked him to." She then explained how for days she'd been asking Archangel Raphael to help her. Mary's story was her sign that he'd heard her prayers. There was no doubt he was there. The energy in the room was palpable.

Ever since that day, Mary has worked with archangels Raphael and Michael. Each time she asks them for their aid, she feels their energy in the room. She knows Raphael came that day to serve and reassure her client, but she can't help but think he also came to introduce himself as someone who could be of great assistance. Mary feels blessed to have had the experience.

Mary's story is similar to other accounts I've heard from massage therapists and bodyworkers who learned about angels by working with clients. And the reverse is true, too: clients who feel and see evidence of Raphael during their healing sessions often become believers.

For example, a reflexologist who asked to be identified as Karen G. calls upon Archangel Raphael to send healing energy through her hands and into her clients. Karen says, "Some of my clients have said they see a green glow coming from my hands before a reflexology session. Others have said they've seen the healing energy ball come at them during our sessions, and that this energy makes them feel better."

These days, many hospitals employ energy healers, such as an Angel Therapist named Tae Takiguchi Basta who works in a Hawaiian hospital. Tae recalls working with a patient who had severe pain in his foot. In her mind's eye, she saw Archangel Raphael touching the patient's heart and sending him healing energy. She never touched the patient during this session.

Afterward, the patient told Tae that he'd felt as if someone was touching his body. Yet each time he'd open his eyes during the session, no one was there, and Tae was sitting across from him. She didn't tell him that it was Archangel Raphael. After the healing, he was free of pain.

Raphael Helps Healers

Part of Archangel Raphael's healing work involves supporting health-care professionals. Raphael partners with healers in an effort to bring wellness to the world's population. If your heart is drawn toward the healing arts and sciences, then you'll want to work closely with Archangel Raphael every step of the way.

Here's a wonderful prayer to say if you're considering pursuing a career in health care:

> *"Dear Archangel Raphael, thank you for guiding my healing work on every level. I ask for your clear guidance in selecting modalities to study, support for my studies, and personal help so that I open up to the highest levels of my God-given abilities. Please assist me in fully opening my mind, emotions, and spirit to Divine healing energy; and allow me to be a perfect conduit for healing in all ways."*

If you're already employed in the health-care field, you can say this prayer to bring Archangel Raphael into your healing practice:

> *"Dear Archangel Raphael, thank you for employing me in a wonderful healing career and for clearly guiding me to the best outlets and opportunities to serve as a healer. Thank you for supporting me in all ways and for sending wonderful clients and projects to me. I now fully awaken and open my God-given healing channels, and allow Heaven's beautiful healing light to stream through me."*

If you're a healing professional, Archangel Raphael guides you in several ways, including helping you:

1. Select a healing specialty—for example, he may push books related to healing off of bookshelves

2. Find an appropriate school or training facility for you to attend

3. Pay for training and schooling, including arranging for time off work, transportation, babysitting, and so on

4. Set up a private practice or gain employment at a wonderful healing center

5. Obtain clients and patients and ensure that you're paid for your work

6. Conduct your healing work, including giving you instructions as you're working with patients

7. Receive healing projects, such as teaching opportunities, ideas related to writing articles or books, and charity work

If you need help with any of the preceding aspects of your healing career, be sure to ask Archangel Raphael for assistance. Remember that he can't violate your free will and must wait for your express permission before he can guide you. The words that you use to request this help are secondary to the action of asking for aid. Raphael just needs your sincere request and he's on the case.

Once you ask for his assistance, Raphael will take action in the same modes that he uses for healing. In other words, he will either give you Divine guidance in the form of ideas you have about your healing work; effect a direct, immediate intervention; or offer a gradual intervention.

Raphael will help you in the way that's best suited for your situation and life purpose. Trust this powerful archangel to support your healing work . . . in every way.

Laypersons Performing Healing with Archangel Raphael

Please don't conclude from this chapter that only trained professionals have success with calling upon Archangel Raphael to heal others. Raphael comes to anyone who sincerely wishes to assist with another person's (or an animal's) healing.

Sophia Fairchild was traveling in western Ireland when she first felt the full force of Archangel Raphael's powerful healing abilities. She was touring with a group across the Burren, which is a 100-square-mile plateau of limestone rock that looks very much like the surface of the moon. This mystical landscape contains dozens of Celtic crosses, ancient fortresses, and megalithic tombs. Although its surface appears smooth, the Burren is full of dangerous potholes.

Cold wind howled across the open plain, so most of the group turned back to seek shelter. Only three people remained on the Burren: a couple and Sophia. Then Sophia watched with horror as the middle-aged man slipped and fell awkwardly into one of the deep potholes.

Sophia recalls what happened next:

He lay immobile, obviously in great pain. Shouts for help went unanswered as the fierce wind swept all sound away. The man groaned and began lapsing into shock. We were in the middle of nowhere, with no help of any kind. As his wife ran back across the plateau to seek assistance, I found myself alone with an injured stranger.

I knew I must stay with him and offer some kind of aid, but had no idea what to do. He was a German doctor who spoke little English. I was someone with no medical training who'd never done any kind of healing before and spoke no German. He pointed to his hip and said, "Kaputt," meaning that it was broken. Not knowing what else to do, I gently placed my hand on his leg and began praying that healing energy would flow through me to him.

As soon as I did this, I sensed the presence of Archangel Raphael with us. I could feel the angel sending powerful green healing light to the site of the injury, and was surprised to find myself the conduit for this powerful flow of healing.

It wasn't so much that I saw this energy as the color green, but rather that there was a green *feeling* surrounding the archangel's presence. His aura felt like the soft, refreshing atmosphere of a cool waterfall in a lush rain forest. It was as if a fountain of vitalizing healing force was being poured down upon us, funneling into the body of the man lying on the rocks.

I smiled at the German doctor, and he smiled back at me in silence. He too could feel the comforting presence of the angel as he drifted in and out of consciousness. Then the doctor's wife returned with a blanket, saying that a rescue team was on its way.

After this experience, I began to train as a healer. Archangel Raphael had demonstrated to me that instead of using our own energy to heal, we need to step out of the way and allow the greater powers of healing to flow *through* us. This not only prevents us from becoming depleted, but ensures that the energy being sent to the other person is of the highest vibration.

Studies show that all forms and denominations of prayers have measurable healing effects. Your prayers can lead to miraculous results! And there's evidence that the greater the number of people who pray, the more powerful and faster the healing effects.

When you hear about anyone whose health is compromised, the best way to help is through prayer and guided action. Worry never helped anyone, but prayer *always* does.

Laurie Montanaro's friend asked for prayers for his sister-in-law, who had fallen from a horse and severely injured her head. The doctors had given her a one percent chance to live.

Laurie had never met the woman, but she immediately asked Raphael to surround her with green healing light, and continued to do so daily. Then a miracle occurred: her friend's sister-in-law awoke from her coma, started physical therapy, and was released from the hospital.

Laurie says, "I'm totally convinced that Raphael had worked his healing on her, along with like-minded people who sent out positive prayers for her recovery."

Like the small child whose single voice saves the Who world in Dr. Seuss's classic *Horton Hears a Who*, your prayer can tip the balance in favor of a miraculous healing. You can also contact prayer groups at your local religious or spiritual center or on the Internet to solicit additional prayers.

Archangel Raphael can cure any physical malady, and in the next chapter we'll look at the emotional and psychological healing support that he also offers.

CHAPTER FOUR

EMOTIONAL HEALING

"Dear Archangel Raphael, I now open my mind and heart to you and ask that you infuse me with faith, hope, and happiness. Please help me feel safe and secure about my present and future life. Please help me be willing to release old unforgiveness and anger. Please help me clearly see solutions and possibilities. Please help my mind and emotions be healthy in all ways. Thank you."

Some healing modalities hold that every illness or injury has an emotional basis. And certainly it's true that illness and injury create emotional upheaval. Life can seem even more stressful if your body is in pain or you have to suffer through medical tests and frightening health prognoses.

"Mental health" means the ability to feel happy and safe. Clearly, when life throws you a surprise, it's normal to react with fear or anger. In a well-adjusted person, these feelings gradually subside as the individual adapts to the changes. There are healthy and unhealthy coping mechanisms.

For example, a healthy coping behavior would be talking with supportive friends, exercising, meditating, or praying. An unhealthy or self-destructive coping mechanism would include drug or alcohol abuse. The distinction lies in whether or not the coping behavior enhances health and happiness.

Archangel Raphael can heal your emotions, as well as your body. As with other aspects of working with God and the angels, you must first give permission before Heaven is allowed to intervene in this way. Also, Raphael's emotional healing follows the same pattern as his physical-health methods, which include the following three avenues:

1. **Divine guidance.** You receive intuitive instructions about action steps to take that will lead to the healing you're praying for. This guidance can come in the form of having a great idea, repetitive thoughts, a dream, signs from above, or gut feelings.

2. **Immediate, direct intervention.** You pray . . . and the next thing you know, you feel better.

3. **Gradual-direction intervention.** You pray and over time you feel better.

As a former psychotherapist, I can attest to the power and effectiveness of the angels' emotional healing. In fact, the most common comment I hear from people who begin working with angels is: "I feel so much more peaceful, happy, and safe now." Those feelings are the foundation of mental and emotional health.

Healing Away Fears, Phobias, and Anxieties

Fear is a silent thief that robs us of peaceful moments. It steals away the ability to enjoy the present moment, and has us nervously wondering what bad event is on the horizon. Fear attracts negative experiences with its low energy.

Worry is related to fear. The angels once taught me that this emotion draws to us the very thing we're worried about. The angels said, "Instead of worrying, pray. Worry makes things worse, while prayer makes things better."

Everyone feels worried and afraid at times, and it's a normal response to life stressors. Fortunately, Archangel Raphael can alleviate fears so that ordinary stressors are less . . . well, *stressful.* For example, most people are afraid of feeling pain at a dentist's office. A woman named Jenny decided to work with Archangel Raphael to alleviate this anxiety. She says:

> I call upon Archangel Raphael when I am at the dentist's office awaiting a filling or even a cleaning. When I sit in the chair, my mind starts to spin out all the possible pain and problems that could occur, and I become tense and panicky.
>
> So I'll ask Archangel Raphael to help me, and I suddenly feel him hold my hand. A sense of peace envelops me, and I immediately relax. The visit is over quickly, and the pain is minimal. I even heal faster than the times I forget to call upon Archangel Raphael. This also works for visits to the doctor's office and medical tests.

Phobias are another form of fear that attaches to a specific item (clowns, for instance, or snakes) or condition (heights or closed spaces, for example). Since phobias usually originate from a frightening experience, Archangel Raphael removes the fear energy from that originating event.

For instance, a woman named Nan Fahey was phobic of thunderstorms, so she was very frightened when she found herself driving in one. As the storm raged on, Nan had the presence of mind to ask Archangel Raphael to be with her.

Nan recalls:

> Although I was the only person in the car, I felt Raphael's hands on my shoulders, and they stayed there until I got home. His touch gave me comfort and made me feel calm despite what I'd just been through. Since then I haven't been bothered by thunderstorms, and I attribute this to Raphael.

Phobias occur when we feel unable to control the object of our fears. This experience healed Nan's former phobia, since she now feels more in control, knowing she can call upon the angels anytime she's afraid. You can do the same for any phobias that may be limiting you by asking Raphael to help—for example, through this prayer:

> *"Dear Archangel Raphael, thank you for dissolving the fear related to my past and present experiences with* [describe the object of fear]. *I ask that you help*

*me feel peaceful and safe in these circumstances, with
the knowledge that you are always with me."*

Panic attacks are anxiety based and involve debilitat-
ing feelings—such as the sensation that you can't breathe
and that you're dying of a heart attack. After the first
episode, the person usually develops a phobia of having
subsequent panic attacks. This fear then compounds and
sometimes *triggers* new ones.

Diane Fordham had suffered from anxiety disorder
and panic attacks for many years. Her attacks, which usually occurred in the middle of the night, frightened her.
She'd wake up feeling as if she couldn't breathe, with her
heart racing madly.

One night in desperation, she decided to ask Archangel Raphael for help. Diane recalls:

I silently called to him, *Please, Archangel
Raphael, I'm terrified and feel like I can't breathe
and can't think straight. Please help me!* I felt his
presence and found myself taking deep breaths.
I slowed down, and my thoughts fell back into
place. I relaxed and was able to lie back down in
my bed and go to sleep! Thank you, Raphael!

Like Diane, Lukas Tobler, whom you read about in
Chapter 2, was healed of panic attacks with the help
of Archangel Raphael. Lukas had his first panic attack
when he was a passenger on a high-speed train, and he
continued to have them thereafter. Lukas was very afraid
of dying of a heart attack or stroke during these attacks.

Although Lukas was aware of angels, he attempted
to solve the issue with what he calls "more rational

psychological methods." So he tried taking antidepressant medication, but that actually made him feel worse.

Finally at Christmastime, still shaken by the ongoing panic attacks, Lukas called out to Archangel Raphael and his helper angels, asking them to please free him from this agony. He immediately felt Archangel Raphael surround him with comforting energy. This made him feel safer.

Within two weeks, the frequency of Lukas's panic attacks was reduced to a few scattered moments of mild anxiety. Knowing that Archangel Raphael and his helper angels were always there for him gave Lukas a great sense of appreciation, relief, and hope. Within six months, his panic attacks ceased altogether without any further medical assistance.

Here is a prayer to ask for help in healing panic disorders:

"Dear Archangel Raphael, please send your emerald green healing energy to my mind, heart, and nervous system. I ask that you soothe, comfort, and reassure me. Please help me forgive my past, and know that I am completely safe and protected."

Healing the Heart

Archangel Raphael heals both the physical and the emotional heart. No matter what the source of pain, he provides comfort and care.

Here are some prayers for various situations calling for emotional support and healing:

Prayer to Heal a Grieving Heart

"Dear Archangel Raphael, please send your emerald green healing light to my heart. Help me feel whole again. Please restore my hope, faith, and trust so that I can move forward in my life. Please reassure me that everyone involved in this situation is watched over by the angels. Thank you."

Prayer Following a Relationship Breakup

"Dear Archangel Raphael, my heart needs your healing help, please. Help me let go of fears and hurt feelings; adjust to my new life without my partner; and release sadness, loneliness, unforgiveness, and anger. I ask that you surround me completely with your healing green light to clear and shield me. Thank you."

Prayer to Overcome Disappointment

"Dear Archangel Raphael, I need a strong, comforting hug from you now. Please reassure me that this experience is ultimately for the best, and that something even better is on the horizon for me. Thank you for healing my heart and mind of any ego involvement so that I can detach from drama and fear-based ideas. Help me trust in God's perfect plan for me and my loved ones. Thank you."

Prayer to Release Anger and Resentment

"Dear Archangel Raphael, thank you for bathing my heart and mind in your purifying emerald green light, washing away all lower energies, toxins, and hard feelings. Thank you for lifting my mind so I can gain a bigger perspective on everything and not take others' actions personally. Please guide my actions and thoughts so that they reflect my true spiritual nature of Divine love. Thank you."

Prayer to Overcome Worry or Anxiety

"Dear Archangel Raphael, please wrap your arms and wings around me and give me your strong reassurance that my loved ones and I are safe. Help me trust my inner feelings and take action accordingly. Help me detach from other people's opinions and clearly hear my inner voice of truth. Please give me clear guidance and ideas as to the next steps to take to heal this situation. Thank you."

Healing Emotional Exhaustion and Burnout

If life seems difficult or trying, you may become emotionally exhausted from constant struggles and unrewarded efforts. This can lead to burnout, which is the process of feeling numb, apathetic, and chronically tired.

Kelly Roper felt completely burned-out a few years ago. She was physically, emotionally, spiritually, and mentally exhausted; and overwhelmed by life circum-stances. As she recalls: "I was surrounded by negative people, situations, and darkness as I struggled through a divorce and family deaths. I couldn't see light anywhere in my life."

In desperation, Kelly appealed to God and Archangel Raphael for help. She received immediate guidance to meditate and listen to gentle, relaxing music. Kelly says, "During meditation I experienced a vivid daydream: Surrounded by darkness, I saw a bubble of light floating toward me. Inside the bubble was a young man who held out his hand to me, guiding me to him, and we danced together inside the light. I believe this man was the arch-angel Raphael. The vision was so strong!"

Afterward, Kelly felt relief from the burnout. She finally felt peaceful, relaxed, and uplifted—her prayers were answered! She says, "I look back in amazement and gratitude of the wonderful gift that I received in my dark-est hour."

Like Kelly, you can ask for and receive spiritual heal-ing to revive your energy and outlook. Here is a prayer for healing:

"Dear God and Archangel Raphael, thank you for reigniting my passion for life. Thank you for helping me enjoy each moment and face any challenges with grace and excitement. Please guide me to be strong, to speak my truth, and to stand up for myself when necessary. Thank you for giving me the energy and perseverance to meet my responsibilities and still stay true to myself."

The Healing Path of Forgiveness

A great deal of Archangel Raphael's healing work comes from his releasing of built-up toxic energies—chiefly, stored anger and unforgiveness. The healing workbook *A Course in Miracles* clearly states that all forms of illness stem from unforgiving thoughts. Virtually every religious and spiritual path advocates forgiveness as a necessity of healthy living.

So how do you forgive the seemingly unforgivable? How do you let go of anger when someone's actions hurt you?

The first step is to decide that you're willing to consider forgiveness as an alternative. As long as you're set against forgiveness, it can't occur. Some people hang on to resentment because they want to punish the offending person. Yet, who's really punished if you're holding toxic and acidic anger within your mind and body? Just a tiny bit of willingness to forgive can open the doorway wide enough for the angels to enter and effect an emotional healing.

Once you've allowed some willingness to forgive, the next step is to ask for assistance. Here is a helpful prayer:

> *"Dear God and Archangel Raphael, I am willing to forgive* [person's name] *and myself for this situation, in exchange for inner peace. I am willing to take responsibility for the role that I played in this situation, and I ask for help in truly learning the life lessons involved in this challenge. I am no longer willing to carry the burden or toxins of anger in my mind and heart. I now fully and freely give these*

judgments, thoughts, and feelings to you for purifica-
tion, detoxification, cleansing, and transmutation."

Your body will likely react to this prayer as the angels release toxins from your physical being. So you may experience shakes or shivers during the cathartic process. This is a positive sign that your cells are releasing old energy, helping you feel lighter and freer.

There's a healing reason why virtually every religious and spiritual path strongly recommends forgiveness. Here are some spiritual texts and scriptures with inspirational words recommending forgiveness that show the universality of this important healing step:

> *"There can be no form of suffering that fails to*
> *hide an unforgiving thought. Nor can there be a*
> *form of pain that forgiveness cannot heal."*
>
> — *A Course in Miracles* (New Age)

> *"You shall not take vengeance, nor bear any*
> *grudge against the sons of your people, but you*
> *shall love your neighbor as yourself."*
>
> — Leviticus 19:18 (Judaism)

> *"Then Peter came and said to Him, 'Lord, how often*
> *shall my brother sin against me, and I forgive him? As*
> *many as seven times?' Jesus said to him, 'I do not say to*
> *you up to seven times, but up to seventy times seven.'"*
>
> — Matthew 18:21–22 (Christianity)

> *"Where there is forgiveness, there is God Himself."*
>
> — Adi Granth (Sikhism)

"Subvert anger by forgiveness."

— Samanasattam (Jainism)

"The superior man tends to forgive wrongs."

— I Ching (ancient Chinese)

"Bear no grudge."

— Treatise on Response and Retribution (Taoism)

"He who forgives and seeks reconciliation
shall be rewarded by God."

— Qur'an 42 (Islam)

Now that we've covered the scope of Raphael's healing for adults, let's look at how the archangel supports and helps children as well.

CHAPTER FIVE

HEALING CHILDREN

*"Dear God and Archangel Raphael, please watch over my chil-
dren and ensure their health and safety. Please guide me to be
the best parent possible and provide for all of their needs."*

I've always believed that Heaven gives top priority to
children, and that the angels do their best to keep them
healthy and safe. In cases where adults are mistreating
children, I believe the angels must feel frustrated that
they're unable to violate those abusive adults' free will.
Still, the angels do their best to watch over the children
of the world.

Archangel Raphael seems to hold a special place in
his heart for children. His healing work is welcomed by
young, pure hearts that accept his gifts with grace and
gratitude.

In this chapter, all but one of the children's names
have been changed to protect their privacy. The adults'
names are all real (as they are in the entire book). The following stories are particularly poignant since the kids see
and feel Raphael's presence during their healings because
of their trusting nature and open minds.

For example, Ruby Niecke was with her nieces, ages 12 and 14, at her lake cottage. In the evenings, they'd share *Archangel Oracle Card* readings with each other. The eldest niece, Fiona, kept pulling Archangel Raphael cards, so Ruby shared as much information as she could about the healing angel.

The last afternoon of their vacation, a bee stung Fiona's left foot. Ruby took the girl's foot in her hands and said, "It's okay . . . let's call upon Raphael. Take deep breaths in and out, and he will heal you."

Fiona said, "He's with us!" and then her crying stopped and she said, "Oh my God, Auntie Ruby, the pain is gone!"

Then Fiona started to dance in a twirling motion while singing, "Thank you, Raphael! You healed my foot!" Her perfect faith in the angels allowed her to receive this instant healing. We can learn so much from children's examples!

Conception

The Bible recounts how angels supported the pregnancies of Sarah, Mary, and Elizabeth. These are examples of the ancient connection that angels have to helping parents with every aspect of childbearing, childbirth, and child raising.

I've received several stories of women successfully conceiving after they asked the angels for help. In fact, my own parents were having difficulty getting pregnant, until they put a prayer request in to their church's prayer ministry . . . and I was conceived three weeks later. So I naturally believe in the power of prayer, since it was the beginning of my physical origin!

An Angel Therapist named Morgen Drasnin was preparing her client to do in vitro fertilization and implantation. The client had been unable to conceive naturally, and she and her doctor had concerns about her body's ability to successfully carry the pregnancy. So Morgen invoked the presence of Archangel Raphael.

Morgen psychically saw Raphael place his hands on her client's lower abdomen and hip bones, and stream an enormous amount of energy and light into her body. At one point, Raphael motioned for Morgen to place her hands on her client's hip bones in the same way.

When the work was done, Morgen asked her client to share any experiences she had during the session.

She began, "After you put the heating pad across my abdomen . . ." and went on to share her thoughts and visions.

Morgen smiled, and told her that it wasn't a heating pad she'd felt, but the immense love and healing energy of Archangel Raphael!

Her client is now eight months pregnant and going strong. Morgen says, "Thank you, Raphael, for balancing my client's body and creating the perfect conditions for her successful pregnancy."

Traditionally, Archangel Gabriel is the angel to call upon for help with conceiving and pregnancy, since he's the one who announced the conceptions of Mary and Elizabeth in the Scriptures. When you work with both Gabriel and Raphael, you bring in the twin energies of the nurturing and maternal angel (Gabriel) and the healing angel (Raphael). What a winning combination!

Here's a powerful prayer for conceiving a baby:

"Archangels Gabriel and Raphael, I call upon you now to usher in the soul of my beloved unborn child and help my womb be a wonderful temple where my baby can grow healthy and strong. Please guide me clearly as to actions that I and the father of the baby can take to ensure a successful conception and healthy, full-term pregnancy."

Pregnancy

Archangels Raphael and Gabriel watch over pregnancies, ensuring the safety and health of both mother and baby. The archangels give intuitive guidance to help mothers know the most beneficial actions to take for themselves and their babies. The archangels guide health professionals and healers involved with the pregnancies as well.

An Angel Therapist named Barbara Iñiguez invoked Archangel Raphael when a friend experienced complications during her pregnancy. The condition worsened, and she was about to lose her baby, so she had to be on complete bed rest, unable to get up at all. She asked Barbara to call upon the healing angels on her behalf.

Barbara says:

So I wrote down a prayer asking Archangel Raphael, Mother Mary, and Heaven to help her heal and let her and her baby be safe. She said the prayer on a daily basis, and even memorized it. Her health was restored, and she had a healthy baby boy two months later. She was so grateful to Archangel Raphael that she printed the prayer and gave copies to everyone she knew.

Here's Barbara's prayer:

"Dear God, Holy Spirit, and Archangel Raphael, I ask that you surround me with your loving healing energy. I ask that my physical body enjoy complete health and that the illusion of disease be freed from it. I ask my body to act according to Divinity's plan. I ask that Mother Mary, being the loving Universal Mother, come to my assistance; I lay my maternity in her loving hands so she protects my baby. I ask that this situation be solved in a miraculous way. And so it is."

I admire this mother's presence of mind, which allowed her to ask for Barbara's help and then to say the prayer regularly. It's important that we take the human action steps given to us by the angels through our intuitive thoughts and feelings.

Here's another prayer for a healthy pregnancy:

"Dear God, Archangel Gabriel, and Archangel Raphael, thank you for overseeing every aspect of my pregnancy, ensuring my child's and my own safety and health. Please protect us fully and guide me and my physician clearly about which steps to take to enhance our health and well-being. Thank you for helping me honor my own body, as well as my child's growing body, with healthful foods and beverages. Thank you for ensuring that I am immersed in and

surrounded by loving, gentle, and supportive people and situations. Thank you for helping my pregnancy be completely healthy and full-term, with a safe delivery of my baby."

Adoption

Archangels Gabriel and Raphael can also help parents successfully adopt a wonderful new family member.

Here's an effective prayer for adoptive parents to use:

"Dear God, Archangel Gabriel, and Archangel Raphael, I call upon you now. I ask that you guide me through the adoption process. Please guide me to the best agency and resources, and bring our child to us easily and peacefully. Help me remain strong, positive, and patient through this process."

Here's a healing prayer for birth mothers to say:

"Dear God, Archangel Gabriel, Archangel Raphael, and Mother Mary, thank you for watching over me and my baby during my pregnancy. Please guide my heart through these strong emotions and help me cope and, where needed, forgive. Thank you for guiding me to an honest and caring adoption agency, and helping my child become successfully adopted by loving and caring parents. If it is in my child's best interests, please help me continue to be in my child's life."

Early-Childhood Healings

The angels are with your children every moment throughout their lives (just like they're with adults such as yourself!). Young toddlers sometimes have mishaps as they explore their world, but fortunately Archangel Raphael is there to catch them should they fall.

Donna's two-year-old granddaughter Kristy burned her head and face when she reached for her mother's teacup. So Donna and the rest of the family immediately called upon Archangel Raphael to heal the little girl without scarring.

Doctors initially thought Kristy might need skin grafts, but they first had to clean her up and cut her hair so they could assess the damage. Then they wrapped her face in bandages and transferred her to a children's-hospital burn unit three hours away. Donna and her family prayed that archangels Raphael and Michael would protect and heal Kristy.

Donna remembers: "Sometime during the night, I felt the angels around me and knew everything was going to be fine. With this reassurance, I fell asleep."

The next morning, the doctors who removed Kristy's bandages were stunned, as her skin was only red, with no signs of blistering or shredding. They said it was a miracle that she didn't need surgery! Kristy was sent home, with a one-week follow-up visit scheduled. And on that visit, doctors said she was all clear. As they'd all prayed, Kristy was healed. She's now seven years old, with no scars and no signs of trauma.

Donna says, "I've always believed in the healing powers of Archangel Raphael, and this was validation that when you believe, miracles really do happen."

In addition to accidents and injuries, Raphael can heal children of illnesses. At the first sign of a sniffle, call upon the archangel with this prayer:

"Dear Archangel Raphael, please help my child [name] heal right away. I ask that you please surround my child with your healing green energy and help my child be completely healthy and well, now."

Janet Stevens experienced Raphael's loving healing power when she called upon him for her 18-month-old granddaughter, Caity, who'd been ill for months with fevers over 105 degrees. One day when Caity wasn't well, Janet drove to see her and found the child sitting unresponsively on her mother's lap. Her eyes showed that she didn't feel well.

So Janet put her hand on Caity's back, closed her eyes, and took some deep breaths. She asked Archangel Raphael to come to the girl and heal her. Janet pictured his emerald green light going from her hand and into Caity's body and Archangel Raphael vacuuming out the virus inside of her.

A few hours later, Caity asked for something to drink and eat, which was remarkable since she'd barely consumed anything during her illness. Janet knew that her virus was gone. Soon Caity was running around the house playing, happy and healthy.

As a parent or grandparent, you naturally feel upset when your child falls ill. So you can also ask Archangel Raphael to ease *your* heart and mind to keep you calm as you help your child. Here's a prayer to use:

"Dear Archangel Raphael, please reassure and calm me about my child's health. Please help me to accurately hear your guidance and be able to think clearly, and act swiftly, to help my child feel well fast. Thank you."

As a pediatric nurse, Carmen Carignan was acutely aware of the horrible implications when her four-year-old son Matthew became very ill with a heart infection. The lining around his heart was inflamed, with an accumulation of fluid that was life threatening. He was transported by ambulance to the large medical center 60 miles away from their home.

The pediatric cardiologist said that if Matthew's condition worsened that night, he would be transferred to Children's Hospital Boston to be placed on a heart and lung machine. Carmen was almost paralyzed with fear and disbelief. This couldn't be happening!

The nurses escorted her to a small room across the hall, where she could lie down while they conducted tests on Matthew. It was in this room that Carmen screamed in anguish and pleaded to the universe that she didn't want to lose her son. She fervently prayed and called upon Archangel Raphael to go to Matthew and assist him in any way he could. Carmen had no choice but to hand over the entire ordeal—and surrender her son and the situation—to God.

Carmen sobbed uncontrollably. Through her sobbing, she heard a door open and close, as if someone had left her side and walked out. Overwhelmed with grief, she didn't think much of it. She tossed and turned, unable to sleep as her mind raced on.

In the morning, the cardiologist brought Carmen to Matthew's room. Through his moans, he seemed more peaceful somehow. The cardiologist looked intently at her and said, "I don't know what happened, but Matthew is showing signs of improvement. Maybe it's prayers; I don't know."

Carmen says:

At that moment, I knew it was Archangel Raphael. I realized that when I'd called upon him, he had come to me, then left to be with my son—hence the door opening and closing. Once more, emotions gripped me, but this time I was filled with love and gratitude when I realized that a miracle had occurred. Matthew was in the hospital for two weeks. He gradually improved every day. He's now a grown, 18-year-old young man about to graduate from high school.

Carmen's fervent prayers brought immediate help for herself and her son. When you pray, make sure that you're focused 100 percent on your desire. Use your whole mind, emotions, and body when you pray. Be completely sure that you want, and know that you deserve, what you're praying about. If you hold back even a little, thinking, *Well, I'm not sure I deserve Heaven's help,* you'll slow or block the answer to your prayers.

Fortunately, most parents are totally sure that their children deserve Heaven's healing treatment. So their prayers are particularly effective.

Catherine Fleay's three-year-old daughter Julia had been sick for weeks, with no sign of improvement. She had a lingering cold, mucus, a bad cough, and earaches. She was miserable and couldn't sleep.

One night as Catherine and Julia were reading a bed-time story, they decided to ask Archangel Raphael to help heal her. They both asked for his aid and pictured him putting his wings around her in bed. Julia then lay there, and they both visualized breathing in the color green.

The next morning Julia appeared slightly more alert and energetic. Catherine dropped the girl's older sisters at school and was driving to the supermarket when Julia exclaimed, "Mummy, look at the little green lights!"

They were driving on a bushland stretch of road with no traffic lights. Julia very animatedly was pointing in front of her, just behind the front seat. So they said hello to Archangel Raphael and thanked him for the healing. Julia was very excited about that.

They continued driving to the store, where they were both excited to see a huge pallet of green olive-oil tins with the brand name "Raphael." They laughed and said to the archangel, "We got the message—thanks again!"

Julia healed quickly over the next couple of days and was soon back to her beautiful, laughing and energetic self. To this day, she calls upon the angels.

Experiences such as these help children know that angels are real and trust that they can call upon them for help with their health and other life areas. When a child is instantly healed, everyone's faith is boosted, which is another form of healing.

Healing Childhood Fears

In the previous chapter, we looked at how Raphael allays adulthood fears, worries, and phobias. Well, he does the same for children. If you were like most kids, you probably had fears about monsters hiding in your bedroom at night. Tia Spanelli recalls how Archangel Raphael helped her to overcome this childhood fear:

When I was a little girl, I was afraid to go to bed at night because I thought that a monster was going to get me. I watched movies, and my imagination ran wild. The only place I felt safe was in my grandmother's room.

One night I was sleeping there, but I still felt a little uneasy. I kept waking up and going back to sleep throughout the night in my grandmother's king-size bed. I woke up yet again to see an extremely tall figure in a green cloak, with his hands folded in prayer. He was standing on the side of the bed in front of me. I squinted my eyes, but everything seemed to be clear.

Between his strong, manly looking hands was a long peach-colored rosary that seemed to stop next to his knees. I didn't see this tall gentleman's face; it was like a light mist near his head. His cloak or robe appeared very long, thick, and dark hunter green. It had ripples in it and was decorated with a tan line going across the bottom half.

The tall gentleman never said anything, but I felt reassured and I finally slept well. After that, I had no more fears.

At such a young age, I didn't understand what I'd experienced. It wasn't until years later when I read some of Doreen's books that I realized I had been visited by Archangel Raphael and that he eased my fear of the dark and going to sleep. His presence was calming and reassuring, as if I'd been healed from my fears and they just vanished away.

These days children are more apt to see departed people in their bedrooms because parents are more supportive of their offspring's clairvoyance. So, beyond the days of imagining monsters in the closet, today's children are afraid because they're really seeing beings in their rooms at night (similar to the little boy in the movie *The Sixth Sense*).

You can empower your child to alleviate this condition by teaching him or her to call upon archangels Michael (who clears away lower energies, including Earthbound spirits) and Raphael (who heals the emotions and mind when one is afraid).

My CD called *Chakra Clearing* is also an invocation of Archangel Michael, who thoroughly clears the energy of homes. Just play it in the room that you want cleared. You can leave if you like and just let the CD play continuously while you're gone. Parents tell me that their children love this CD.

Here's a powerful prayer that you can copy and put in your kids' bedrooms for them to use if they become afraid:

> *"Archangels Michael and Raphael, please come to me now. Please clear this room of all low energy and help me be happy and calm. Thank you for protecting me and everyone in this home."*

Raphael Helps Schoolchildren

As children grow up and go to school, Archangel Raphael is still their steady companion. Raphael keeps schoolchildren happy, healthy, and focused upon their classwork. Alexandra Laura Payne also found that Raphael helped her pass an important exam.

The night before her test, Alexandra began to suffer from an excruciating migraine headache. Her face felt numb; and she was nauseated, her body was drenched in a cold sweat, and any movement or noise sent an agonizing pain through her head.

As she curled up under a blanket, Alexandra desperately called upon Archangel Raphael. Immediately, she sensed his gentle, soothing presence at her bedside. She felt like she was lifted onto the softest, fluffiest white clouds. In her mind's eye, she saw Raphael's hands performing caressing-like motions over her forehead and face about half an inch above her skin. The archangel's hands emanated the most gloriously soothing white light. She could feel a palpable physical sensation as this light touched her skin.

Alexandra relaxed into the healing, completely trusting Raphael. The next morning as she went to her exam, she'd never felt better. She wasn't a bit nervous, and she achieved the top grade! Alexandra credits all of this to Raphael. She says, "He was truly a miracle to me that night."

Archangel Raphael soothes the mind so that students can think clearly. A boy named Alex was intensely worried about an upcoming school exam. He knew that worrying would interfere with his ability to concentrate during the test, so he decided to ask Archangel Raphael for help. Alex says, "The moment I finished my prayer, I had a very powerful sensation of peace and calm. I stopped worrying, and I didn't have any mental blanking during the test and was very confident in my abilities."

In addition to Raphael's soothing qualities, students can also call upon the two "intellectual archangels," Uriel and Zadkiel. Archangel Uriel helps with mental functioning so that the mind is sharp and focused. Archangel Zadkiel has long been regarded as the angel of good memory so that students can remember all of their facts, figures, and formulas.

Here's an effective prayer for students to invoke all three archangels for their school exams:

"Dear Archangel Raphael, thank you for calming my mind, emotions, and body so that I am confident and relaxed. Dear Archangel Zadkiel, thank you for helping me easily, accurately, and clearly remember all of my study materials and class teachings. Dear Archangel Uriel, thank you for helping me think clearly, comprehend the test questions' meanings, and be able to focus and concentrate with ease. Thank you, Archangels, for helping me complete this exam quickly and accurately, with a top grade."

In the next chapter, we'll look at how Archangel Raphael heals our appetite and cravings so that we only desire healthful food and beverages.

CHAPTER SIX

DIET, ADDICTIONS, AND EXERCISE

"Dear Archangel Raphael, I am ready to release [name the addiction]. *Please cut my cords of fear connected to this addiction and fill my body with your loving and soothing emerald green light. Thank you for shifting my cravings so that I only desire healthful foods and beverages. Thank you for completely disconnecting me from unhealthful cravings. My heart, mind, and body are now totally filled with love."*

Archangel Raphael's prescriptions, like those of any good physician, include his recommendations for a healthful lifestyle. So when we pray for healing, Raphael's answer may include intuitive guidance to become chemical free, to eat healthfully, and to exercise regularly. Fortunately, he also heals cravings so that you begin to desire life-affirming foods and beverages.

Archangel Raphael certainly helped *me* overcome my own addictions to wine and chocolate, which I was emotionally and physically dependent upon. I didn't want to give them up, but Raphael's strong guidance was that these two substances were the cause of my severe edema (swelling and fluid retention) and headaches. His message was clear: I needed to give up the offending substances that were the cause of these conditions, and then I'd be healthy.

But I worried about how I'd handle the withdrawal and cravings. After all, I was in a daily cycle of consuming wine and chocolate. I'd previously been hooked on strong coffee, too. But Raphael had miraculously removed my cravings for coffee—headache free!—when I'd asked for his help, and ever since I hadn't wanted any more.

For this reason, I trusted Raphael to fully support me as I committed to giving up wine and chocolate. I told him, "If I don't want these substances, then giving them up will be easy." As soon as I gave my nod of approval, Raphael was able to work with my freewill choice and effect a healing.

In my mind's eye, I saw and felt him working in between my two physical eyes in the area of the pituitary gland or "third-eye chakra." He seemed to snip a thin umbilical-cord-like appendage from the front of my third eye. I saw waves and sparkles of emerald green light . . . and then it was over.

Since that day, I haven't craved chocolate or wine at all. I thought for sure that when I went to see the movie *Chocolat* with Johnny Depp, my cravings would return after watching celluloid images of melting chocolate. But there were none then or since. To me, the elimination of cravings is a true miracle. Thank you, Archangel Raphael!

In this chapter, you'll meet other people who have had their unhealthful cravings healed by Raphael and learn how you, your loved ones, or your clients can also benefit from the archangel's help.

Healing Chemical Dependency

I worked as a chemical-dependency counselor and psychotherapist in various outpatient and hospital-based addictions programs (including the famous CARE Unit) for many years. I'd attend 12-step programs with my patients and also for my own addiction recovery. Groups such as Alcoholics Anonymous, Narcotics Anonymous, and Al-Anon are remarkably effective support systems for those who are ready to heal their addictive tendencies. I love and appreciate that the 12-step model is based upon spiritual faith in a Higher Power. Working with Raphael and the 12-step programs is a powerfully effective combination for healing addictions.

Studies show the efficacy of prayer in reducing or eliminating addictive tendencies. Over the years, I've talked to hundreds of people who worked with Archangel Raphael to eliminate dependencies on drugs and alcohol.

The prayer at the beginning of this chapter is extremely effective in stopping addictive cravings. I've received testimonials that this type of prayer has healed people from addictions to many types of drugs, including alcohol. Usually, the prayer results in the substance having a nauseating effect, so the person then pairs the addiction with unpleasant feelings.

That is exactly what happened when a woman named Lesley worked with Archangel Raphael to heal her marijuana addiction. Lesley had been addicted to this drug for about 12 years. She used it to numb the feelings and negative self-talk stemming from sexual abuse in her childhood. She also relied on it to relax during her premenstrual time, when she'd normally feel stressed. Lesley was able to go for about a week without smoking, but then she'd frantically search until she could buy some more marijuana.

One day a friend loaned her the book *Angels 101*. Lesley read about the assistance that the different angels give and saw that Raphael helped with overcoming addictions. So one night after she went to bed, Lesley asked the archangel to help her overcome marijuana cravings.

The next afternoon she had a smoke, and it felt awful. Lesley was conscious of the negative effects and noticed that it stopped her from focusing, and lowered her energy. She didn't like the "head fog" feeling it caused.

That was the last smoke Lesley had. It's been many, many months, during which she hasn't had any cravings for marijuana, nor has she thought about using it. It just isn't a part of her life anymore. She doesn't want it, and she feels free!

Lesley says:

> I believe that Archangel Raphael showed me what marijuana really does to me when I had that last smoke, and that what I thought were the benefits were just an illusion. I think he removed it from my energy field so that I no longer think of it or crave it. My premenstrual times have been easy, and my mood has been calm. I believe he healed this for me as well.

Archangel Raphael can't violate someone's free will, so he can only heal addictions if the person *wants* to be healed.

So the live-in boyfriend of a woman who wants to go by her initials, SMH, must have been ready to give up marijuana when SMH called upon Raphael.

SMH had just finished my angel course in Australia, which caused her to examine her entire life for areas of low energy. She realized that her boyfriend's daily marijuana smoking was bringing both of them down.

SMH asked Archangel Raphael to surround her boyfriend with healing green energy, knowing that the angel couldn't interfere with a person's free will, but hoping that her boyfriend wanted to free himself of the bonds of addiction.

SMH says:

> A miracle occurred. The very next morning my boyfriend woke to inform me that he'd smoked his last joint. Just like that. We'd had countless arguments and endless discussions about his habit for years, with no result. He'd quit for a while, and then he'd be straight back to his habit at the first opportunity. Why, then, did he quit out of the blue? The answer lies in the power and love of Archangel Raphael.

While SMH hasn't told her boyfriend about her prayer, it gives her great comfort to know that when you pray, God and Archangel Raphael will do all they can to help.

Cigarettes and marijuana create psychological dependency, as well as physical cravings. People believe that they *need* these substances in order to relax and feel good. They self-medicate their emotions and energy levels with chemicals.

A man named Claudio Moreno started smoking cigarettes when he was 17, as he thought they'd calm him down and make him appear older and more interesting. When he went to college in a foreign country two years later, he also started smoking marijuana.

When Claudio was packing to fly home during a college break, a friend gave him a small ceramic statue of Archangel Michael to ensure safe travels. Claudio threw the statue in his suitcase, without any padding or protection. Upon his arrival, though, he was surprised to find that the statue was still intact. His original intention had been for it to be destroyed so that he'd have an excuse to throw it away.

The fact that the statue was undamaged motivated him to have mental conversations with Archangel Michael. To Claudio's initial surprise and disbelief, Michael responded in many different ways! Claudio received the strong intuitive knowledge that the archangel wanted him to quit smoking. But he wasn't ready.

And then, after graduation, somebody else gave Claudio a small statue of Archangel Raphael, which made him lose all doubt about the angels' power. He knew that Michael was introducing him to Raphael. At that point, Claudio was still smoking. Although he realized that he was addicted, he had no desire to quit. The hope of one day leaving smoking behind was long gone in his mind. Claudio didn't care about his lungs, but Raphael did.

Every time the issue would come up, Claudio would push Raphael aside. Deep down, he knew that he was killing himself. A longtime athlete, he was aware that he was getting to a juncture where he'd have to make a choice. But the choice scared him so much that he started to get injured while training. During those downtime periods when he was recovering, Claudio was pleased that he didn't have to choose between smoking and athletics. He would just sit in his room and smoke time away.

But once he returned to sports, the injuries became more frequent. So did his warnings from Raphael. Claudio recalls, "I knew he was trying to save me, but I was just thinking, *If I have to die, so be it.*" The signs started getting stronger. Then his girlfriend left him because of the smoking. He still didn't care; in fact, he smoked even more after she left.

One night Claudio had a terrible nightmare: that his smoking had destroyed his family, business, friends, and life. He woke up sweating, and he took his stash and flushed it. Claudio then went back to his room and looked at the archangel statues. He felt terrible about what he'd done to his body for all those years. He started to cry and gazed at Raphael. Claudio knew he was there; he could feel him.

Claudio implored Raphael to please fix his mind so that he'd be strong enough to quit smoking. The first days, Claudio prayed a lot, and Raphael never left his side. He heard the archangel say to him: *You have Michael; you have me. Don't numb yourself . . . you have a road to travel.*

Since that moment, Claudio has released his fears to the angels. His injuries from training stopped, and the level of his performance in sports increased. The next several months were easier, and his life started to improve. He made more friends and got another girlfriend. Claudio says, "I owe my life to archangels Michael and Raphael."

Healing Codependency

When you love an addict or alcoholic, you often endure unhealthy situations, which may lead you to blame yourself for the love one's addictive behavior. This is compounded if the addict also blames you for the chronic drug or alcohol use, since those in the throes of addiction rarely take responsibility for their actions.

Having been married to an alcoholic and marijuana addict, I know the pain of codependency firsthand. Those of us who are rescuers and who want everyone to be happy are particularly vulnerable to the codependency malady. Our codependent behavior actually reinforces our loved ones' addictions in a process called *enabling*.

Fortunately, help is available in the form of the excellent international support group Al-Anon, books such as *Codependent No More* by Melody Beattie—and Archangel Raphael.

A woman named Jill received help from Archangel Raphael as she navigated the channels of healing from codependency and her husband's alcoholism. During an angel reading, she was told to stop ignoring the pressing issues in her life. She believed her main problem was her husband's alcoholism, which was worsening daily. Some angel books were recommended to her, and she learned about Archangel Raphael.

So while her husband was out drinking, Jill would soak in saltwater baths and meditate on Archangel Raphael and ask him to help her. She noted that Raphael's energy was very peaceful and calming and concluded that it was better than any drug that a physician could prescribe.

Jill asked Raphael to heal her husband. She recalls that after her prayer . . .

> . . . boy, did things start happening! My life went crazy to the point where I'd feel bitter toward my angels. As I started asking for help, my life was falling apart. Tragedy after tragedy kept happening. But now that I look back, it was a blessing. I now realize that these tragedies had to happen in order for my husband to heal. It was a wake-up call for the both of us.

Her husband tried to commit suicide and also got two drunk-driving tickets within two months of her prayer. Jill and her husband separated but still talked. She reminded him to ask his angels and God for guidance. She, too, continually asked for help.

Her husband soon hit rock bottom when he was in an accident and rolled his truck. It was a miracle he didn't get injured. He became even more depressed than he had been before, yet he was unwilling to try anything.

Jill's prayers were answered when she met with a friend who was a recovering addict, and he referred them to an addiction-recovery program. Jill could feel Archangel Raphael guiding them to the right people.

This is when their lives started changing for the better and the family healing began. Jill and her husband attended support meetings several times a week, and they loved everyone they met in the program. She believes Raphael helped them find the right group. Her husband has been sober for several months, and they're back together. He's a new person: laughing, joking, and having fun sober.

Jill says, "These last months have been the happiest I've ever had. I owe it to all my angels but especially to Archangel Raphael. I hope my story can help other people ask Raphael for assistance and receive the happiness I've received."

Increased Desire to Exercise

I love exercise and how it makes me feel. When I'm working out, I can feel stress peeling away and being replaced by euphoria. Afterward, I feel centered, calm, and ready to face anything. I can't imagine life without exercise!

Exercise is a healthful habit that requires motivation and some self-discipline. Those who are busy, sedentary, or stressed may not think that they have enough time or energy for physical activity. Yet, if your angels are nudging you toward fitness, then Heaven will help you all the way. Archangel Raphael knows that exercise is an important component of physical, mental, and emotional health. So naturally he's willing to help with giving you every form of support for your workout program . . . including igniting your motivation and desire to exercise!

Darlene always viewed exercise as a chore until she asked Archangel Raphael for help. The change was almost immediate, and now instead of dreading her workouts, she looks forward to them. Her stamina also improved, and she now exercises five times a week, instead of her previous twice-a-week regimen.

Darlene says:

Raphael is guiding me to do more yoga, and I'm seeing the benefits. Now if I go two or three days without a workout, I miss it and don't feel as well. So, it's a completely different mind-set. I just know that Raphael is helping me with exercise, diet, and my health. It's absolutely amazing how much Spirit reaches out to us if we just ask for help.

If you'd like to have more motivation to exercise, here's a wonderful prayer to say:

"Dear Archangel Raphael, thank you for igniting my passion to exercise healthfully and consistently. Thank you for guiding me to develop an exercise program that suits my interests, schedule, abilities, and finances. Thank you for helping me truly enjoy exercising my body."

A High-Vibrational Diet

A long time ago, the angels told me that everything that we eat or drink has corresponding effects upon our spiritual and physical health. They taught me that every food and beverage has a vibration that the body absorbs. High-vibrating foods and beverages help increase a person's energy levels, awaken psychic abilities, and are healthful. Low-vibrating ones have the opposite effect.

Foods and drinks vibrate according to how much "life force" they have. *Life force* refers to how "alive" the food and drink is.

Think of foods and drinks as either being alive or dormant. An example of alive foods would be fresh fruits and vegetables. As the produce wilts over time, it loses its life force and becomes lower vibrating until the life force is dormant (dead).

Anything that supports life force is high vibrating, so foods that are freshly picked and prayed over have the highest vibrations. (Try this experiment: Take a sandwich and cut it in half. Pray over one half of the sandwich only. Then compare freshness of the two halves within three days to see how much longer the prayed-over one stays fresh.)

Processes that reduce life force include: canning, freezing, cooking, microwaving, steaming, dehydrating, freeze-drying, and frying. Any process that would hurt or kill a person will also affect the life force of fruits, vegetables, nuts, and grains.

Any food that has been treated cruelly will maintain that negative energy within it, and your body will absorb the low vibrations when it's consumed. So animals that are mistreated on "factory farms" yield low-vibrational meat, eggs, and dairy products. You can pray over these foods to raise their vibrations, but it's so much better to choose animal products from humane farms.

In the same vein, pesticides are extremely low vibrating, as these substances are used to kill *(-cide)*. So choose products that are organically grown to ensure that you're ingesting the highest-vibrational foods and beverages. Juicing releases the life force from fruits and vegetables unless the juice is drunk within 30 to 60 minutes from the time of juicing. Again, think of any other living being and ask if it could survive in a blender? That's exactly what happens to fruits and vegetables.

So the highest-vibrating meals consist of freshly picked organic fruits, vegetables, grains, and nuts. Many people on the spiritual and health paths are adopting "raw diets," something that I wrote about in my book (with co-author Jenny Ross) *The Art of Raw Living Food* (Hay House, 2009).

So if you're getting intuitive thoughts or feelings to switch to a more vegetarian diet, that really is the angels speaking to you. Archangel Raphael and the other angels guide you to the healthiest lifestyle that supports your life purpose, well-being, and happiness.

Lisa J. Livingston asked Archangel Raphael to show her how to be more in tune to him, and how to raise her own intuitive vibrations. She immediately saw a vision of two words: *caffeine* and *gluten*. Lisa was hooked on caffeine-laden energy drinks, and she loved bread and pasta.

The following morning, she had a double dose of liquid vitamins and mangosteen, lots of water, and a banana. It was a combination she maintained for a week, and to her complete amazement, she never experienced any nervousness or headache from the lack of caffeine. Now caffeine free, Lisa says that she feels wonderful and has no more cravings for bread and pasta, thanks to Raphael's able help.

In addition to improving your diet for spiritual reasons, many people ask for angelic dietary guidance for health purposes. Each night Carol Clausen asked Archangel Raphael to improve her eyesight and hearing so that she could work as a prekindergarten teacher. Soon afterward, her desire for meat simply disappeared, and her cravings for vegetarian food increased. She now mostly eats raw fruits and vegetables.

Carol believes that her prayers changed her appetite and that Archangel Raphael helped increase her income so she could easily afford organic food. She now happily works in a prekindergarten, as she'd dreamed of, and says that her new diet has improved her health.

I've watched dietary changes create amazing positive shifts in people's health and behavior. The jury is in: what you eat and drink affects your wellness, mood, longevity, and energy levels. When my sons were preadolescents, I began serving them only organic vegetables, and I was amazed that their boyish aggressiveness vanished. They became gentler as I fed them gentler food. *Super Size Me* is a powerful movie that documents how food affects us psychologically and physically. I highly recommend it!

When Melanie Orders was waiting for an ambulance to take her to the hospital due to a gallbladder attack, she heard a voice say, "You're going to be okay; just get some pressure on the area by leaning over the bench." Although in immense pain, Melanie followed the instruction. "Breath, just breathe; they'll be here soon," the voice said.

The ambulance arrived and took Melanie to the hospital. Although she was afraid, the voice kept reassuring her that everything would be okay. It continued to calm and stay with her throughout her hospitalization. Every night Melanie could feel an emerald green presence sending healing light into her gallbladder. She knew this was Archangel Raphael!

Melanie continued to work with Raphael after she returned home; and she was guided clearly to change her diet by drinking water with lemon juice, eating more fresh fruits and vegetables, and avoiding wheat and dairy products. She also switched to eating fish instead of poultry and was guided to drink pineapple juice as her sweet treat.

She lost nearly 40 pounds on her Archangel Raphael–guided diet. She also received intuitive knowledge of how old anger had stagnated within her gallbladder. Now Melanie works as a massage therapist to help others release stored anger from their bodies, with the help of Archangel Raphael.

The Angel Diet for Busy People

The fast-food industry was created for people who don't have time to cook. When you're too busy to make your own meals or sit down at a restaurant, it's easier to buy a fast meal at a drive-through place. Fortunately, Archangel Raphael helps busy people navigate the travails of healthful eating on a tight schedule.

Natasha Hoar's job requires lots of driving and overnight travel. Since she puts her work ahead of eating healthfully, she never made the time to prepare healthful meals to take on the road. Instead, she'd eat fast, fatty foods that were tasty but left her feeling bloated and sluggish. Natasha also began suffering with aches in her right side.

Finally, she asked Archangel Raphael to help her eat better (although she told him that she was only willing to eat healthier food if it tasted good!). Almost immediately, she went from craving sour-cream-covered quesadillas to desiring lower-fat vegetarian meals. She even lost the taste for beef burgers, which was amazing considering Natasha's work takes her into restaurants and fast-food chains specializing in hamburgers!

Instead, she tended toward vegetarian burgers and dishes. Once a big tuna fan, she now has no taste for it at all, which means an environmental advantage for the oceans, since the overfishing of tuna has left the fish nearly extinct. Natasha has discovered amazing little restaurants that specialize in organic products. This subtle switch leaves her feeling lighter and more energized after meals.

Natasha says:

> One of the best side effects of this experience is that, with my healthier diet, I can hear and feel the angels much more clearly. I marvel at how asking for help, and being open to receiving it, made such a fantastic change in my life. I'm thankful to Archangel Raphael and all of the angels for their unwavering support and efforts.

Not only do busy working adults benefit from Raphael's dietary advice, but so do students who also tend to fall prey to the fast-food industry (which shamelessly sells its unhealthful wares as school lunches). Fifteen-year-old Stevie's schedule would put even fast-track adults to the test: waking up at 6 A.M., going to school until 4:30 P.M., eight hours of sports a week, and adult-education evening classes.

Sleep deprived, Stevie barely had enough energy to get through each day. After learning about Archangel Raphael, she asked him to guide her food and beverage choices and clean up her diet. She specifically asked him to help her eat more fruit, drink water instead of soda, and consume less junk food. After two nights of appealing to Raphael, Stevie developed cravings for oranges and apples. She had previously never touched fruit, and now she was eating it three times a day!

Stevie continued talking with Raphael every night and thanked him for all of his help. Her eating habits totally changed for the better, and she drank lots of water and forwent soda. Her cravings for fast food vanished. Stevie says, "At school my friends would offer chocolates or chips, and my body simply denied them. I had no desire for any of it at all, and this surprised me. My family would offer me soda, but I had no desire for this either—my body wanted water instead."

Stevie's energy and stamina increased, and she was no longer tired in the mornings. Her attitude became happier, which friends and family complimented her on. Throughout the experience, Stevie knew she had free will. She says, "My appetite changed because I allowed Archangel Raphael to help me and guide me to the right choices, and whether or not I chose the right thing was entirely my decision."

Stevie has likely inspired her friends and family to eat more healthfully by her positive example. In this way, she is an Earth angel, spreading Raphael's message of health far and wide.

Archangel Raphael is a multifaceted and multi-talented healer, as we've seen from these amazing testimonial stories. A true healer, he helps anyone and everyone in need . . . including our beloved animal friends, as we'll explore in the next chapter.

CHAPTER SEVEN

PROTECTING OUR PETS

"Dear Archangel Raphael, thank you for watching over, healing, and protecting my pets. Please help [name of pet(s)] *be completely healthy and happy. Please guide my actions so that I can support my pets' health."*

Archangel Raphael has unlimited healing abilities. He can be with everyone who asks for healing simultaneously, assisting each being individually. Talk about multitasking!

Raphael is brilliant at helping animals live safe, happy, and healthy lives. One day my beloved Himalayan house cat Romeo climbed onto the roof and refused to come inside. I was running late for an appointment, and I couldn't assure his safety. So I asked Raphael to help, and within a minute, Romeo walked happily toward me, purring as I placed him indoors.

I've received dozens of similar stories of Raphael retrieving lost pets quickly and mysteriously. One woman even said that after she'd asked the archangel to bring her lost cat home, the kitty appeared at her front door with body language as if she were being pulled into the house by an invisible leash!

Raphael responds rapidly to all calls for healing support, whether it's for a human or an animal. Steve Wood discovered this after finding his five-pound American hairless terrier, Dandy, with her head down, coughing. Thinking she'd gotten something stuck in her throat, Steve gently patted her back.

Still Dandy continued coughing and seemed to have difficulty breathing. So Steve opened her tiny mouth and tried to look down her throat, but could see nothing wrong. He held her body in a vertical position, with her head at the lower end, and tapped on her back. But still nothing was expelled, and her breathing seemed to be getting increasingly shallow and labored. Now Steve was worried, almost to the point of panic. He was just about to grab his car keys and head for the nearest veterinarian's office when he suddenly remembered Archangel Raphael!

Steve had frequently asked Raphael to heal the battered and emotionally damaged dogs rescued by his wife's organization. He'd seen some miraculous recoveries. But in the panic of the moment with his own dog, he almost forgot to ask for the archangel's help.

Holding Dandy with both hands, Steve could feel her labored breathing. She could only draw very short, shallow breaths; and she was becoming woozy from lack of oxygen. Steve blurted out, "Raphael, please help her!"

Dandy suddenly relaxed and began breathing normally! She didn't cough again. Nothing was expelled. She just started breathing normally through her nose. Steve sat holding her, with tears streaming down his face, while thanking Raphael.

Strong, Clear Prayers

As in Dandy's story, Raphael seems to respond immediately to prayers for a pet's health. This is similar to the instant healings that children often receive after their parents call upon Archangel Raphael. This immediacy occurs when the prayer is strong, clear, and committed.

Some people pray halfheartedly for themselves because of fears about whether they "deserve" Heaven's help or not. They worry that they haven't been good enough, or are concerned about whether it's okay to "bother" God with requests or if asking for help is allowed.

But these fears are cast aside when they pray on behalf of a beloved child or pet. In such cases, their inner mother bear is channeled into a protective and confident prayer: "We need this healing, and we need it now!"

Lest you think that demanding a healing from Raphael is blasphemous or disrespectful, please know that the angel teases out the true essence of every prayer—whether it's said in anger, sadness, frustration, or peace. Archangel Raphael, being egoless, is nonjudgmental. He loves everyone unconditionally. He would never refrain from answering a prayer, but he would be blocked if you weren't asking for a healing with 100 percent commitment.

So in any prayer request, please be certain that your thoughts and feelings are completely aligned, and that you're absolutely certain that you desire (and know that you deserve) the answer to your prayers. Those are the factors that ensure immediate help.

Here's a prayer to say if you need assistance in aligning your thoughts and feelings in the same direction:

"Dear God, Archangel Raphael, and Archangel Michael, I now open my mind and emotions to you. Thank you for clearing away fears and insecurities, helping me know that Heaven loves me and wishes to bestow its healing grace for my peace and happiness."

Prayer's effectiveness for humans, animals, and plants is now well documented in the scientific literature. Studies on animals are troubling, since scientists intentionally inflict wounds on laboratory subjects to study prayer's effects on healing. This methodology would never be tolerated in human studies.

Nonetheless, the results are heartening. The most recently cited nonhuman prayer study came from Loma Linda University in 2006, when researchers tested the effects of long-distance intercessory prayer on 22 monkeys. The monkeys were the breed "bush baby" from Africa, who had reacted to the stress of being caged by overgrooming themselves to the point of making their skin bleed.

Scientists asked an experienced prayer group to pray for half of the monkeys, using the animals' names. The handlers were unaware which monkeys were being prayed for to avoid influencing the study's outcome.

The monkeys that were prayed over had measurably smaller wounds compared to the others. The prayed-for monkeys also had higher red-blood-cell and hemoglobin counts (indicators of healthy blood). The differences between the two groups was statistically significant, meaning that the effects of prayer were greater than you would expect to find by chance.

As a double-blind study, this research is considered important scientific evidence of the efficacy of prayer, and its ability to positively influence health and healing.

An Angel Therapist named Kate Whorlow intensely asked Archangel Raphael to heal her pet cat's newborn kitten, who was barely breathing and was lying limp in her hands.

Kate's cat, Lily, brought her the kitten soon after he was born, dropping him into her hands as if to say, "Please help!" Lily anxiously licked the tiny kitten, but he was unresponsive. Still in the middle of giving birth to the rest of her litter, Lily needed Kate's help.

So Kate petitioned Raphael to please heal the kitten to make sure he lived. She asked Raphael to pour his healing energy into the kitten's heart and lungs to get the heart beating so that he could breathe.

After about ten minutes, the kitten started moving and then suckling from Lily, who by this time had given birth to her next kitten, who was also feeding happily. Kate was so relieved! She thanked Archangel Raphael for the amazing healing that had just taken place. She named the kitten Angel, and he's now a healthy five-year-old cat.

Kate's prayers were strong, clear, and lifesaving.

The Written Prayer

Writing your prayer on paper, or printing one from this book or another source, is also highly effective. The written prayer is a talisman and reminder to say the words repeatedly until the answer comes either in the form of a healing or as intuitive guidance about taking action steps to elicit the desired outcome. I've had excellent results from writing a prayer in the form of a letter to God, and then leaving that paper facing upward on my prayer mantel.

Nicola Kimpton wrote her prayer for her pet guinea pig's health and placed it where she could see it as a reminder to continue praying. Her guinea pig Bully was ill, with raspy, labored breathing. The medicine prescribed by the veterinarian worked for a week, but then the guinea pig relapsed.

That's when Nicola implored Archangel Raphael to heal Bully. She wrote a prayer to Raphael on a piece of paper and placed it in a special place where she could see it every day.

Over the next few days, guidance came in the form of thoughts or an inner "knowingness." Acting upon this higher guidance, Nicola made Bully as comfortable as possible and spent extra time with her. She repeatedly told Bully how much she loved her.

Instead of viewing her as sick, Nicola visualized her as healthy and well. When Bully wheezed and struggled, Nicola stroked and soothed her and put her faith in Archangel Raphael.

After a week, Bully's eyes regained their spark, and she was breathing and eating normally as if nothing had ever happened. She was healed, and her owner believed that this was a miracle. Two years later, Bully and her companion guinea pig, Squeak, are still going strong. Every day Nicola thanks God and Archangel Raphael profusely for the love and light the pets bring into her life.

Mutual Raphael Experiences

Archangel Raphael's healing energy is so strong that everyone involved usually sees or feels evidence of his presence. As you've read in the stories in this book so far, his energy creates tingling effects in the body of the person he's healing. Well, when Jann Dring asked Raphael to heal her dog, she also felt the strong sensations of the archangel's remarkable energy.

Following dental surgery, Jann's four-year-old Maltese dog, Kye, developed an abscess under his jaw, requiring antibiotics and dressings. To prevent him from scratching it, the vet put a plastic cone-shaped collar around his head. Kye was very sick and wasn't eating or drinking. He spent most of his day just lying in his bed, barely lifting his head.

As Jann stroked him, she asked Archangel Raphael to heal Kye. She asked that her dog be completely healed, happy, and healthy again as soon as possible. Jann says, "That was when my body tingled from head to toe. I felt warm and relaxed; and Kye wagged his tail, got up from his bed, and walked to his food bowl."

Kye ate, drank, and slept. The next day, his wound had healed, and he was running around again! Now, a year later, he doesn't even have a scar, and Jann gives complete credit to Archangel Raphael.

Perhaps Jann felt Raphael's healing energy because the archangel knew that she was stressed, and pet owners' moods can affect their animals' moods. Jann is also a highly sensitive person who feels energy easily, and Raphael's is *strong*.

Animals definitely sense Raphael's presence. A woman named Karen has a dog, Oso, with lifelong physical disabilities. When she got the dog, she didn't expect her to live long. So each night, Karen asks Raphael to be with Oso and to help her walk outside then and in the morning.

Karen notices that when she calls upon Raphael, Oso looks upward and behind her. Karen believes that Oso is seeing and reacting to Archangel Raphael's presence. Karen, too, sees glowing green lights in her bedroom each evening, evidence of the healing angel hearing her nightly prayers.

How touching that Karen and Jann both experienced Raphael's presence during their pets' healings. Now that's true love!

Over the past seven chapters, we've detailed how Archangel Raphael heals everything and everyone who desires his help. He is the supreme healing angel.

In the next chapter, we'll look at Raphael's other specialty: guiding and protecting travelers.

CHAPTER EIGHT

RAPHAEL, THE TRAVEL ANGEL

*"Dear Archangel Raphael, please accompany me and
my loved ones on this journey. Please ensure everyone's
safety, comfort, and health throughout the entire trip.
I ask that you connect me with loving and helpful people
during the journey and also help me bring blessings to
fellow travelers. Please keep all aspects of the journey
smooth, harmonious, and peaceful. Please help me with
[name specific details with which you'd like assistance].
Thank you for overseeing my travels in all ways."*

In the Book of Tobit, a canonical text accepted by the
Roman Catholic and Eastern Orthodox churches, Archangel Raphael (disguised as a human nobleman) accompanies Tobit's son Tobias on a long and arduous trek by
foot. Tobias gains wisdom, valuable experiences, and a
bride along the way, thanks to Raphael. Ever since he
accompanied Tobias on his journey, Archangel Raphael
has been a patron saint of travelers.

My work as a spiritual teacher has taken me around
the world several times, and I credit God and Archangel
Raphael for making my journeys safe and peaceful.

Raphael is the ultimate traveling companion who handles all of the small and large details, because his mission is to ensure our well-being. In this way, we avoid the stressful moments of travel that could negatively impact our health.

Remember that Raphael, like God and all of the archangels and ascended masters, is an unlimited being. So he's able to help everyone simultaneously with all aspects of your traveling. Raphael knows that lots of small stressors add up to big, health-threatening stress. So he accompanies you on your travels in order to shield you from needless stressful situations. He is the Angelic concierge!

However, because of human free will, Raphael can only intervene if you give him permission to help. So it's a good idea to call upon him—for example, using the prayer at the beginning of this chapter—before starting any journey.

I've certainly asked Raphael to help me with small and large travel details! After a long flight, the last thing travelers want to hear is that their hotel room isn't available. I've stood at many front desks, talking with the clerk while simultaneously having silent discussions with Archangel Raphael. Always, he exceeds my expectations and unlocks the doors to effortless travel.

Smooth Flights Ahead

As a flight attendant, Philippe Slimbroeck sees the results of calling upon Raphael every day. Philippe always connects to the archangel and his personal guardian angels before each flight. He visualizes them surrounding the airplane with white and green light. This gives him a secure feeling, and he knows that everyone on board is in safe hands.

Most of Philippe's trips are to Africa, and poor weather conditions and upset passengers can be found on most flights. Yet ever since he started working with Archangel Raphael and the other angels, Philippe has found that any turbulence or incident with a passenger has gotten resolved in no time!

Philippe hasn't experienced any nonsecure situations on his flights, which to him is the best proof of Archangel Raphael's caring energy. Philippe says, "I'd like to advise the readers—whether you're a flight attendant, a business traveler, or just leaving on a holiday—to call upon Archangel Raphael and your guardian angels before you take off, to protect and comfort you during your trip."

Who else besides me would love to have Philippe as a flight attendant on an upcoming trip? And synchronistically, after he'd sent this story to me, I met Philippe in person at a London book signing the day before I flew to Africa for the first time!

Philippe's invocation of Raphael during air turbulence is highly effective, and I've frequently done the same thing over my years of travel. *Of course* the angels want to smooth rough rides, both to keep us safe and to minimize health-robbing stress!

When the pilot announces that flight attendants need to be seated and everyone must be buckled in to prepare for upcoming turbulence, I always think of

Louise L. Hay's famous affirmation: "That may be true for you, but it is not true for me!"

I then ask Archangel Raphael and his accompanying angels to fully support and stabilize the airplane. In my mind's eye, I can see the angels with their backs and hands supporting the belly and wings of the plane. Always, the pilot comes back on the speaker system and says, "Well, folks, looks like we were able to bypass that storm system, so I'm turning the seat-belt sign back off." That's when I say "Thank you!" to Raphael and the other angels.

A woman named Christina M. Antonetti was already a very nervous flier who didn't like traveling on airplanes at all. So when her flight from Barbados to New York began to bump around vigorously, Christina clutched the arm of her chair *and* her husband's chest. She was stricken with fear, and she couldn't imagine another five hours of this turbulent flight.

Silently, Christina summoned Archangel Raphael and asked him to please go under the plane, keep it steady for the remainder of the flight, and gently place it safely onto the runway in New York. In her mind, she held a clear vision of Raphael under the plane, his arms above his head, holding it steady.

This vision not only calmed her anxiety, but the turbulence stopped immediately! In fact, it was the smoothest flight she'd ever experienced, and the landing was even better. Before leaving the airplane, Christina thanked Archangel Raphael silently and felt a warm smile spread across her face.

On-Time Travels

If you've ever experienced unexpected delays while traveling, you know how frustrating they can be. And if you have tight airline connections, a delay can mean missing your flight. Fortunately, Archangel Raphael can smooth any kinks in your travel timetable.

The exception would be if the postponement is for your safety. In those cases (such as a mechanic needing time to fix the airplane, or avoiding a car accident because you drive a few minutes later), you'll know it's a "Divine delay" if a calmness washes over you after asking for Raphael's help. This calmness will give you the necessary patience and other factors you need to get you to your destination safely.

Elizabeth Pfeiffer was late for work as she headed out of the house to get into her car during a huge thunder-and-lightning storm. She wasn't worried about driving in the downfall, but the bright blast of lightning that covered the sky and the roaring thunder sent her nervously back onto her front porch.

She had to leave for work right then or risk being late, so she dashed to her car under an umbrella. Before starting the ignition, Elizabeth asked Archangel Raphael to protect her en route to work. That's when she heard a voice that was almost like a thought in her head that said: *Wait*. And this message was followed by another one: *Wait five minutes*.

The message was so strong that although she was late for work, Elizabeth decided to trust the guidance. So she waited, but the storm raged on, and the longer she waited, the worse it got. But within five minutes, as the angels had promised, the thunder and lightning were gone and the rain had subsided.

As Elizabeth drove to work, she noticed several areas along the way that had flooded terribly, which added to her relief that she'd listened to the angelic guidance. And she not only arrived at her job safely, but on time, too.

Elizabeth's story is a wonderful example of a Divine delay that was purposeful in ensuring safety. So only as long as it's safe to do so, Archangel Raphael will undo any delays that seem to occur on your journey, as Gérald Ostiguy discovered.

Gérald was traveling to the Toronto airport to catch a plane home to Quebec when the airline called to say that his flight was delayed. The airline had rebooked him on a later one, and he wouldn't get home until well after midnight.

Travel weary, Gérald asked Archangel Raphael for help so that he'd be home as originally scheduled. Gérald then called the airline back, and they booked him on a flight only 15 minutes later than his originally scheduled one! Gérald knew that this opportunity had been created by Raphael, and he thanked him profusely.

I've also called upon Raphael in similar circumstances. Two times when I was flying home to my local airport, which closes early at night, my delayed flight would have meant that the airplane would land at a larger and most distant airport. Both times I asked Raphael to please safely guide the plane to land on time at the local airport. And, of course, the archangel came through like the champion that he is.

And Raphael helps with scheduling other forms of transportation, too! Call upon him to ensure that your train, bus, car, boat, or other vehicle arrives safely and on time. Do keep in mind that everything has Divine timing, and that sometimes when you think you're arriving late, it's actually for a good reason. So if there's a traffic jam when you're driving, just keep affirming that you get to your destination exactly when you're supposed to. You'll either miraculously arrive on time, or conditions will be such that your later arrival is actually better than if you'd arrived punctually. *Trust.*

When Tanya Snyman flew to the U.S. from South Africa to take my Angel Therapy Practitioner course, she experienced Archangel Raphael's traveling help along the way. At London's Heathrow Airport, Tanya dreaded standing in the long line for economy class, so she asked Archangel Raphael to help in this regard. As she neared the check-in section, Tanya was whisked to the business-class counter by a smiling assistant who upgraded her without her even asking (except for asking *Raphael*).

After this experience, Tanya trusted the archangel's travel help even more. The following day when she was coming to my workshop facility, Tanya was delayed at her hotel's front desk. She worried that she'd miss the hourly shuttle bus and would be late to class.

But Tanya checked this worry and changed it to a prayer instead. She asked Archangel Raphael to step in and help her out. She says that after she did so, "it was as though time stopped, and I got on the bus with plenty of time to spare!"

When Tanya says that Raphael stopped time, she wasn't speaking metaphorically. Raphael and the other angels literally can stop the clock if you'll ask for their help in ensuring a safe and on-time journey. The key is to request assistance, suspend all worries or disbelief, and

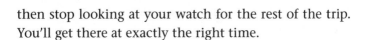

then stop looking at your watch for the rest of the trip. You'll get there at exactly the right time.

Healing and Travel Help

Since Archangel Raphael's two specialties are health and travel, it makes sense that he'd combine his talents when a person falls ill away from home. Traveling has its own unique challenges and is stressful enough when you're healthy, so you need high energy and a good attitude to enjoy the journey. If, however, you need an energy or wellness boost while on a trip, just ask the archangel for help, as Kim Turton did when her son fell ill on a Mexican vacation.

Kim was home in Canada when her 26-year-old son Scott called from Mexico, sick with a bad cold, which progressively got worse over the next few days. By the time he called his mom to tell her about his illness, he could barely walk and just wanted to come home.

Concerned that he might have a really nasty flight back to Canada, Kim sat down and asked Archangel Raphael if he could please help Scott make it to the plane and help him get home safely. She asked Raphael to wrap Scott in a warm blanket of green healing energy and bring him home.

The next day, Kim picked Scott up at the airport. He looked great and said he felt completely better. Kim knew that Archangel Raphael indeed had been listening, and had in fact taken extremely good care of her son. No matter how old our kids are, they're still our babies, and you can call upon Raphael for your children of any age!

When you're requesting that Raphael help you with your trip, it's a good idea to also ask him to protect your health in a prayer such as this one:

"Dear Archangel Raphael, thank you for watching over my journey and keeping me and everyone involved safe, protected, and healthy. Please ensure my high energy, positive outlook, and patience during this trip. I ask that you guide me clearly as to how best to take excellent care of my body. Thank you for protecting my health and keeping me vital and well in all ways."

For Nicholas Davis, Raphael seemed to work double duty, both in securing him an airline seat and helping him recover from an illness. Nicholas was excited to return home to Greece during a political campaign that subsidized airline tickets for Greeks who wanted to travel to vote in an election. Nicholas was a student in Germany at the time, and he arranged for eight tickets for himself and friends. He'd been ill lately and thought that a visit home would be healing.

But when Nicholas went to pick up the tickets, everyone else in his group had one except him! The clerk couldn't explain what had happened, but he also couldn't help Nicholas get a ticket because all of the other airplane seats were booked for the entire week.

Nicholas was devastated! The only thing he could do was pray. So he did with all his heart and soul and asked God, Archangel Raphael, the Virgin Mary, and all the saints for help in getting home to his family.

Around 4 A.M., the phone rang. When Nicholas answered it, there was a lot of noise in the background, and all he could hear was his name and that he needed to be at the airport in five hours to catch a flight to Athens!

Nicholas asked the caller how this could be true, as he didn't have a ticket. The only thing the man said was, "Please, I can't explain. You're on my list, and I had to call you to let you know that you're on the morning flight heading to Athens. When you get to the airport, please proceed to the counter and give your name, and they'll hand you your ticket." And then the man hung up.

Nicholas still doesn't know how he got that ticket. No one at the airline could offer him an explanation. The only thing he knows for sure is that the saints, together with Archangel Raphael and the Virgin Mary, granted his wish, and he had a fabulous time in Greece with family and friends. His physical problems also healed faster than he ever thought they would! Nicholas says, "With the help of angels, life is so blessed and easy!"

So who was the mystery caller who got Nicholas on the Athens flight? I believe it was an angel. I've heard many similar stories through the years, and my conclusion is that angels pay particular attention to airplane travelers because of the high stress and inherent risks involved in this form of transportation.

Nicholas's story is a wonderful example of blended prayers in which he called upon God, Archangel Raphael, and Mother Mary. I've often thought "the more the merrier" when it comes to calling upon trustworthy archangels and ascended masters. If your religious or spiritual preferences are connected with Jesus or a particular saint or deity, then it's a good idea to call upon them for help, in addition to Archangel Raphael.

Archangel Raphael gives full attention to as many people as need his help. His prescriptions are always custom-made for each individual, and his assistance is immediate as long as you ask for it and are ready to receive it.

Lisa Laffargue really needed Raphael after an injury threatened to ruin her holiday travels. Lisa and her husband were preparing to fly to France to visit his family for Christmas when she wrenched her back, her knees buckled, and she fell to the floor. Lisa couldn't move, and the pain was so excruciating that she was terrified that she'd snapped her back.

She cried in pain . . . and out of fear of missing her trip the next day to France. So she asked for help from Archangel Raphael, imagining his emerald light enveloping, and sending healing to, her lower back. Although she awoke in pain the next morning, she didn't give up faith.

Lisa called upon Archangel Raphael again, and suddenly she felt a fluttering sensation across her lower back. She knew this was extraordinary, and that the archangel was healing her. Lisa gingerly got out of bed and started to walk. Although she still experienced some discomfort, her knees didn't buckle, and there was no shooting pain as before.

Lisa says, "The only way to describe this was 'a miracle and healing' from beautiful, darling Archangel Raphael. He healed me enough to be able to get to France for Christmas!"

Isn't it good to know that when you travel, Archangel Raphael is right there with you? What an amazing honor to have Raphael as your traveling companion.

And of course, Raphael is with us throughout every part of our lives, and there is evidence of his steady presence all around . . . if we just notice the signs . . . as we'll explore in the next chapter.

CHAPTER NINE

SIGNS FROM RAPHAEL

*"Dear Archangel Raphael, please send me clear
signs that I can easily notice and understand to let
me know of your presence, and to give me guidance
as to the next step to take. Thank you."*

Anytime you call upon Raphael, he's there. The healing archangel isn't shy or subtle in announcing his presence. He *wants* you to know that he's with you, as a way of comforting you and alleviating stress along your way to a healthy recovery.

Raphael also shows a brilliant sense of humor in his displays of help. An example that always brings a smile to my face is his habit of pushing books off of shelves.

Many people report finding healing books in their homes that they never bought, or discovering ones in their shopping carts that they didn't place there. A long time ago, I bought a much-needed affirmations tape at a grocery store in a discount-cassette bin. Never before or after did I find another affirmations or metaphysical recording in that bin. It was always filled and replenished with old music tapes!

Raphael pushed a book from Joanna Caccamo's shelf to reassure her of his healing presence. Joanna was undergoing a stressful divorce, and it seemed she'd lost everything that was dear to her. When the stress began to affect her health, she wondered which archangel to call upon for help. She then fell asleep.

When Joanna woke up, she found that a book had fallen from her shelves. It was faceup, with a page revealed that she couldn't see from where she was standing. When she went over and picked up the book, she was amazed to find that the page was all about Archangel Raphael!

So she immediately asked Raphael to send his healing energy. In her mind's eye, she saw a beautiful green, pink, and golden light surround her and encompass everything that was within her sight.

The light that Joanna saw is an example of the most common sign from Archangel Raphael. He shines so brightly that people can see flashes or sparkles of his emerald green light with their physical eyes. Yolanda Mendez saw this, along with Archangel Michael's signature purple coloring, after she called upon both angels for help.

The day of her granddaughter's birthday party, Yolanda felt ill and was worried that she'd miss the celebration, which she really wanted to attend. So she decided to ask archangels Raphael and Michael for a healing.

Moments later Yolanda opened her eyes and saw a glowing halo of beautiful bright purple and emerald green moving clouds about four feet above her body. The colorful clouds then drifted closer to her neck and chest, floated toward her feet, and finally returned to her neck area.

Yolanda felt very relaxed, calm, and loved throughout, knowing it was Raphael and Michael guarding and healing her body. All of this lasted about 15 minutes, and afterward she rested for another 15 minutes. When Yolanda got out of bed, she was full of energy and was able to enjoy the birthday party.

Raphael knows that if he announces his presence through his glowing green light, you'll immediately relax and start to feel better. The archangel glows brightly, especially when he's busily conducting a healing session on you or a loved one. This green light has a calming effect on everyone in its vicinity. And you can also invoke the green light by visualizing it around anyone or any particular body part that needs healing.

Like a physician with the best bedside manner, Raphael reassures you that everything will be fine. He calms your fears with his soothing energy and by showing you that he's always nearby.

A woman named Faith really needed Raphael's reassurance when her pregnancy went awry and she found out that she'd lose her unborn son, Luke. Faith envisioned his little soul being held in the arms of the angels. She placed her hands on her belly and asked archangels Raphael and Michael to guide him on his journey back to God.

When Faith awoke from anesthesia after the loss, she had an immediate sense of angelic peace that lasted through the day. She also felt Raphael and Michael around her. Faith says, "The peace I felt was a gift from the angels to let me know our Luke was in a better place and made it home to Heaven. I just knew that he was in the arms of the angels."

And on the way home from the hospital, Faith and her husband were listening to the radio and the song "Angel" by Sarah McLachlan played. As she sang the lyrics, Faith thanked archangels Raphael and Michael for holding her son and keeping him safe.

Faith's sign came through auditory means, which was appropriate because she needed to hear that her son was in the angels' arms to reassure her of Luke's passage into Heaven. Raphael and the other angels often "trumpet" their presence through music.

License plates are a favorite way for angels such as Raphael to convey their messages, as in my friend Jill's sign from above. Jill had tried in vain to find prescription glasses to correct her nighttime driving problem, which stemmed from having Lasik surgery. Although her vision is great during the day, at night she sees "auras" of car lights reflecting in her Lasik incisions.

So on her drive home from work recently, Jill appealed to Raphael to help her have perfect vision day and night, near and far. She then requested a sign to validate that the archangel had heard her prayer.

That moment, Jill noticed that the car ahead of her was a Ford Focus, sporting a license plate with the letters "EZC." She marveled at how clearly and rapidly this sign appeared: a car called "focus" with a phonetic message of "easy see." Jill knew that Raphael had heard and was answering her prayer.

Raphael's Name

Raphael isn't shy, as you've discovered through these stories and hopefully through your own experiences with him. He even announces his name to give you extra reassurance and certainty of his healing presence!

A woman named Barbara was driving her car, very upset and almost in tears about an incident that had just occurred. She quietly asked Archangel Raphael to help her quickly so that she could drive home safely. Just then, her attention was drawn to the right, and she gasped as she saw a sign that read: St. Raphael's Junior School.

Barbara almost jumped with excitement, as she knew Raphael was giving her a sign that he was with her. Then she noticed that the next building was called St. Michael's Senior School.

The whole way home, Barbara felt much calmer and peaceful, knowing that these mighty archangels were with her.

Barbara's signs from Raphael and Michael were very clear and immediate so that she'd know her prayers were heard. Sometimes all we need is the reassurance that Heaven does hear and respond to our prayers. So Raphael sends his signature as validation that he's working on your request.

Although he's an archangel, Raphael can be with you full-time, like a guardian angel. Remember that he (like all the archangels) is an unlimited being who can be with multiple people simultaneously. And if your life purpose involves healing, don't be surprised to learn that Archangel Raphael is with you all the time, guiding your training and work.

Rosa Iacono asked for a sign to know which angel was with her while she was reading an angel book on a flight. Well, Archangel Raphael wanted to let her know that *he* was with her: although Rosa hadn't known of anyone named Raphael since elementary school, she saw or heard the name four times within a week of asking about the identity of her angel.

It began right after the airplane landed. First, the clerk at the hotel front desk was named Raphael. Then, Rosa met a Canadian couple on the beach, and the husband's name was Raphael. Then during a poolside party, an announcer called out the name Raphael several times.

It continued even after Rosa returned home, as she met a new woman in her yoga class who introduced herself as Raffaela. Rosa says, "That young lady never came back to class. Maybe she was an angel?"

Yes, I agree with Rosa. I believe that Raphael sends people who are his namesakes (as do Michael and other heavenly beings) like angelic messengers. I remember when I was guided to go to Lourdes, France, to visit the famous healing grotto discovered by Saint Bernadette. As I was trying to decide if I wanted to make the journey, I kept meeting people named Bernadette. I took this as a validating sign; went to Lourdes; and had an amazing, life-changing experience.

And quite often, Raphael shows his sense of humor in the way that he confirms his presence. When a woman named Janet asked for a sign from Raphael, she didn't realize that he'd send a *literal* sign! Janet recalls:

> After reading *Angels 101,* I meditated and asked for the name of the angel who was with me at that moment. I immediately heard "Raphael." I then asked for him to send me a sign to confirm this and waited patiently.
>
> Well, my sign came a couple of days later when I asked the angels to guide me home safely when I was driving. After this prayer, my

attention was drawn to a building on my right, with a sign that read: Pizza Raphael.

I immediately knew this was literally a sign from Archangel Raphael, and I laughed at his sense of humor. This experience helped me know that he and the angels are all around us and are only a thought away when help is needed.

Of course, the most convincing way that Raphael could validate his presence is by physically appearing before your eyes. In the next chapter, you'll meet people who were fortunate enough to meet Archangel Raphael and will learn how his physical presence helped them heal.

CHAPTER TEN

SEEING AND MEETING RAPHAEL

*"Dear Archangel Raphael, I would like to see
and hear you with my physical senses in order to
be healed and guided by you, and to feel and receive
your healing energy powerfully and profoundly."*

Over the years, I've met many people who've been helped by angels in human form. These temporarily incarnated angels sometimes appear as humans who perform superhuman feats such as lifting cars out of snow and saving drowning people, appearing just long enough to help and then disappearing without a trace.

In Saint Paul's letters to the Corinthians, he said that we should be careful when entertaining strangers, because these strangers might really be angels. Perhaps you've met such an incarnated angel. The following are signature characteristics:

- Has an unusual appearance such as intensely colored eyes or a manner of dress that doesn't fit the surroundings

- Knows your name although he or she has never met you before (or discusses personal information that isn't commonly known)

- Appears and disappears suddenly and without any visible form of transportation

- Helps in a miraculous way, or says just the right thing to reassure you

- Can't be located, or there's no record of the person, if you try to contact him or her afterward

A woman named Donna recalls meeting Archangel Raphael physically when her son Nick was hospitalized. The doctors didn't know the cause of Nick's severe pain, so Donna went into the waiting room to gather her thoughts and pray for a miracle.

As she sat deep in thought, a very handsome gentleman wearing a green shirt and tie walked up to her and asked if he could talk to her. Donna didn't see where this man came from. He said that he'd noticed Donna helping her son walk in the hallway. He said that Nick was too young to be that sick and in the hospital. He asked if he could give her the name of a doctor in Toronto who could help. This doctor had a machine that scanned the whole body, all the way down to the cells. This machine wasn't available in the United States.

The man reassured Donna that she'd get answers from this doctor. So Donna took down the name and phone number of the doctor and made the call that night. The doctor agreed to see them that Friday morning before his clinic opened. To Donna's surprise, he said that he already had Nick's name in the schedule. When she asked how that could be, the doctor said that a gentleman had called and made the arrangements, and he'd expected her to call.

At the clinic, the doctor found that Nick had very high levels of arsenic in his liver and lungs. If he'd remained in that hospital for even two more days, he would probably have lapsed into a coma and possibly even died. The doctors at the clinic detoxified his body of the poison, gave him a chain of treatments, and released him later that same day. Nick felt much better and was able to walk!

So who was that man in the green shirt who came to Donna in the sitting room? Donna says, "I truly believe that he was the angel Raphael, the angel of healing."

So do I. And how fitting that Raphael was dressed in green!

Raphael-Apparition Experiences

Raphael appeared physically to Donna because she needed to take immediate action to save her son's life. Sometimes the healing archangel appears to people in need through psychic, rather than physical, visions. His appearance and presence is very real nonetheless.

In August 2000, while Marilyn Hays's husband, Frank, was in the hospital for open-heart surgery, she continually appealed to Archangel Raphael to please heal him and to be there during his surgery.

After one such prayer, Marilyn was sitting in the living room watching television late at night. She was thirsty, so she pushed the mute button on the remote control and went to the kitchen for some water.

Then she heard a male choir singing . . . but the TV was muted, and she was alone in the house! The music stopped; and this big, towering angel in colorful robes appeared to Marilyn on her right side. He said the following words: "I'll be there."

Marilyn recalls, "I was in such awe and so surprised that I could only say the first thing that came to my mind: 'Thank you!'" Then he disappeared, and the male choir started singing again. This whole experience lasted less than a minute.

Nine years later, Marilyn's husband is still alive and doing well. She says, "I know for certain that it was Archangel Raphael who visited me and kept my husband safe and healthy in response to my prayers.

Marilyn had an "apparition experience"—which is a very real angel visitation—in which she saw and heard him speak. Scientists studying apparition experiences say that the salient quality separating true visitations from hallucinations is their more-than-real quality.

Notice how Marilyn was absolutely convinced that she saw and heard Raphael? This is characteristic of those who have had similar powerful encounters with angels. They just *know* that the experience really happened, and they really don't care if anyone else believes them. As a former psychotherapist, I believe that Marilyn actually experienced a visitation from Raphael that helped her husband's longevity.

Psychically Seeing Raphael

Sometimes the visitation is more like a psychic vision than an apparition, as in the case of a woman named

Krisztina Muskovits. Even though her visitation wasn't physically based, she still had a profound experience.

Krisztina was in bed ill with a sore throat. She ached so much that she asked Archangel Raphael to please heal her. Suddenly with her mind's eye, she saw a big light around her and felt his presence.

Raphael was very big and tall, standing beside her bed. He was wearing a green mantle with golden adornments. He had shoulder-length golden, curly hair. Krisztina felt his energy, a healing power radiating and soothing her throat. This energy was thick and emerald green. It took some minutes, and then she felt much better.

Krisztina says, "Raphael's energy was more gentle than I could imagine. During this whole healing process, there was a golden light in my room. But the energy he gave me was green."

Krisztina's sudden healing speaks volumes about the realness of her encounter with Archangel Raphael. However he appears is perfect for the person and the situation at hand.

Sometimes Archangel Raphael and the other angels come to us in our dreams. When we're sleeping, our minds are more open to receiving angelic messages and healing energy, especially if we tend to lead a busy or noisy life when we're awake.

If you have a dream-time encounter with an angel (or other heavenly being), you'll notice that more-than-real quality of true physical-apparition experiences. The colors and emotions will be strong and vivid, and you'll remember the dream long after you awaken.

A woman named Susie had a dream visitation from Archangel Raphael when she was going through a rough time. Susie's spiritual growth was at a standstill, her friendships were falling by the wayside, and all she seemed to do was work. Every night she asked God for guidance because she felt very alone and adrift.

After Susie's prayer, she had a vivid dream of a key opening a door, revealing a beautiful angel with wings, a gown, and flowing hair. The angel announced that he was Archangel Raphael. In the dream, Susie quickly fell to a kneeling position and lowered her head to the floor in reverence. Archangel Raphael knelt down, too.

Then he said to Susie directly, "Never again are you to think that you're alone. If ever you feel this way, you are to look into your heart because God is always there; and we, as His messengers, are there with Him, too. Look no further."

Susie woke from that dream with all of her worries removed. She says, "I know without a doubt that God, Archangel Raphael, and all the angels are always in my heart and are always beside me."

Archangel Raphael hears and answers every prayer, helping unlimited numbers of people and animals simultaneously in custom-tailored and ingenious ways. Whether he responds to your prayer with a personal visit or with intuitive guidance, trust that the healing archangel is handling the situation in a Divinely perfect way.

CHAPTER ELEVEN

HEALING PRAYERS

Archangel Raphael, as with all of Heaven, responds to any form of prayer. You can say your prayer aloud or silently, with formal or casual words, and with reverence or frustration. The words and form don't matter . . . as long as you ask for help, because the angels can't violate your free will and assist without your permission.

Here are some suggested prayers for various body parts, emotions, and life events that may need healing. Please feel free to edit them to fit your own situation and heartfelt feelings. In fact, the more emotion that you put into the prayer, the faster it will be answered. So please put your whole heart, body, and soul into saying yours.

These prayers can also be edited to suit your particular religious or spiritual beliefs, if you would like to direct the prayer to God, the Holy Spirit, Jesus, or a particular saint or deity. Prayers are much more powerful when they reflect your true feelings and beliefs as you're saying the words.

After your prayer, please let go of worrying about or trying to control *how* it will be answered. Instead, trust in God's amazing wisdom and love to create an ingenious solution that's custom-tailored to you and your situation. Let Heaven surprise you in the way that it answers your prayer.

Notice signs and guidance occurring afterward. As you've read in this book, Archangel Raphael frequently answers prayers by whispering suggestions that you hear as thoughts, feelings, dreams, and visions. When you get a strong hunch to take positive action, know that this is an answered prayer. Follow your hunches and they'll lead you to renewed peace.

These prayers can be said at any time to invoke Archangel Raphael's help in maintaining an already-healthy body, too. . . .

*"Dear Archangel Raphael, I am now fully willing to release
my cravings for* [describe craved substance] *in exchange
for true fulfillment, peace, and health. Please dissolve my
unhealthful attachments and adjust my cravings to embrace
life-affirming and purposeful food, drink, and behavior.
Please help me experience the great feelings of God's love."*

*"Dear Archangel Raphael, I ask that you soothe my mind
and nerves with your emerald green light. Help me relax,
and trust that my loved ones and I are safe and protected."*

APPENDIX

"Dear Archangel Raphael, please infuse my appendix with healing energy and light, helping me have a healthy immune system, digestion, and elimination. Thank you for supporting my health by clearly guiding my diet and lifestyle choices."

APPETITE

"Dear Archangel Raphael, thank you for dissolving fear-based attachments to unhealthful foods and beverages now. Thank you for adjusting my appetite so that I crave only healthful items. Thank you for clearly guiding my eating and drinking choices."

"Dear Archangel Raphael, I ask that you surround my arms with your emerald green healing light, dissolving anything that is not of God, and revealing my arms' true strength and perfect health."

"Dear Archangel Raphael, thank you for infusing my entire back with your emerald green healing light and for supporting me fully. Thank you for lending me your gentle strength so that I can stand tall with ease and comfort."

BIRTH

"Dear Archangel Raphael, please oversee my pregnancy and birth, ensuring my baby's safety and health, as well as my own. Thank you for guiding my gentle, healthy delivery in all ways."

BLADDER

"Dear Archangel Raphael, thank you for sending your emerald green healing energy to my bladder and urinary system. I now easily release thoughts and feelings of anger and allow myself to admit my true emotions to myself and others with love."

"*Dear Archangel Raphael, please purify my blood and clear my veins and arteries with your emerald green healing light, restoring complete health and balance.*"

"*Dear Archangel Raphael, thank you for supporting my healthy, strong, and full-functioning bones with your healing presence and energy. Thank you for my bones' complete restoration and healing, which allows me to stand strong and supported.*"

"Dear Archangel Raphael, thank you for infusing my perfectly healthy breasts with your emerald green light, protecting and supporting them in all ways."

"Dear Archangel Raphael, please send your healing energy to my colon and elimination system. Help me to be perfectly healthy and functioning in all ways."

CONCEPTION

"Dear Archangel Raphael, I trust your healing power, which I know is from God. Thank you for opening the way for my healthy conception. Thank you for leading the way so that my beloved child is born healthy after my easy, full-term pregnancy."

DEPRESSION

"Dear Archangel Raphael, thank you for lifting my mind and mood and allowing me to see the blessings and gifts that are in this situation and in my life. Please help me to feel grateful and at peace, and to let go of painful thoughts and feelings."

*"Dear Archangel Raphael, please help my ears to be healthy
and functioning perfectly with your Divine presence and
healing energy. I am willing to release anything hurtful that
I have ever heard, and I am willing to hear the truth."*

*"Dear Archangel Raphael, thank you for infusing
all of my glands with your emerald green healing
light, balancing and harmonizing my hormones
for perfect health and well-being."*

"Dear Archangel Raphael, please unblock and unleash the full power of my God-given energy. Please revitalize and refresh me so that I fully enjoy each and every moment of my life."

"Dear Archangel Raphael, thank you for washing my eyes with your emerald green healing energy, helping me clearly focus and see all of life's beauty and detail."

"Dear Archangel Raphael, please support the health of my feet, helping me stand tall and strong as I follow the path of my soul and my heart."

"Dear Archangel Raphael, thank you for healing my fingers and restoring health and functionality. I now release any and all pain, and fully absorb your healing energy into my hands and fingers."

GRIEF

*"Dear Archangel Raphael, please hold me in your arms
and comfort my grieving heart. Help me move forward and
rebuild my life. Please give me hope and peace."*

GUMS

*"Dear Archangel Raphael, I trust God, and you as God's
messenger, to lead me to the perfect situations that support
and delight me in all ways. Thank you for bathing my gums
in healing energy, guiding me clearly, and giving me the
courage to follow this illuminated path."*

*"Dear Archangel Raphael, please infuse my scalp
and hair with your healing energy, helping it grow
healthfully—with shine, luster, and vitality. Thank
you for supporting each strand with light and love."*

*"Dear Archangel Raphael, please hold my hands
and help me absorb your powerful healing light.
Please help me let go of any and all negativity and
instead embrace love, light, and positive thoughts."*

HEAD

"Dear Archangel Raphael, thank you for helping me forgive myself and everyone who seems to have hurt me. Thank you for helping me reconnect fully with God's universal love and wisdom. I ask that you bathe my head in your healing energy, helping restore me to perfect health."

HEART

"Dear Archangel Raphael, I now fully loosen and release all emotional grips upon my heart. I give any emotional pain to you and God freely and completely. Please surround me with emerald green light, which I inhale into every cell of my heart and cardiovascular system. Thank you for supporting my healthy heart in all ways."

"Dear Archangel Raphael, please help my hips to be healthy, flexible, and fully functioning. I ask that you mend my hips with your healing energy, and help me move forward fearlessly upon the path of joy and my life's purpose."

"Dear Archangel Raphael, thank you for healing my jaw so that it functions perfectly and healthfully. Thank you for helping me chew and swallow with ease and joy. I now release any and all tension from my jaw, knowing that you fully support and protect me in all ways."

KIDNEYS

"Dear Archangel Raphael, please send your emerald green healing light and energy into my kidneys, clearing and healing them completely. Please restore them to perfect health and help me live healthfully."

LEGS

"Dear Archangel Raphael, thank you for helping me stand with strength, walk with ease, and move with grace. Thank you for infusing my legs with your emerald green healing energy."

"Dear Archangel Raphael, please heal
my lips and restore them to their true state
of Divine health and perfect function."

"Dear Archangel Raphael, I am now willing to release any
stored anger or unforgiviness and clear my liver completely
of any effects of my previous lifestyle. Thank you for healing
my liver and ensuring that it functions in perfect health."

"Dear Archangel Raphael, I ask that you clear and heal my lungs completely. I now forgive myself and others for anything noxious that I may have inhaled. Please guide me as to any changes I need to make to ensure my lungs' perfect health and wellness."

"Dear Archangel Raphael, thank you for introducing me to a wonderful romantic partner who shares my interests, goals, and morals. Thank you for giving me faith, courage, and guidance that leads to my happy and healthy relationship."

Mental Health

"Dear Archangel Raphael, please help me think and see the beauty and order in my life. Please help me release pain from my past and worry about my future, and completely enjoy this present moment. Please guide me to focus upon what I am grateful for and give any painful thoughts to God as soon as they occur."

Muscles

"Dear Archangel Raphael, thank you for massaging my muscles with your emerald green healing energy, helping my muscles heal, relax, and mend. Thank you for restoring my muscles to their healthy-functioning levels and helping me enjoy stretching and bending them in my healthful lifestyle."

"Dear Archangel Raphael, please heal my nails quickly and easily, mending the skin beneath and helping the nails regrow in a strong and healthy way."

"Dear Archangel Raphael, thank you for supporting me, helping me be flexible, and allowing me to see all sides of the picture. Thank you for healing my neck and restoring me to full range of motion."

*"Dear Archangel Raphael, please calm, soothe,
and heal my nerves. Please help my nerves function
healthfully. Please surround me with healing green
light, which only gentle energy can permeate."*

*"Dear Archangel Raphael, thank you for healing
my nose completely and thoroughly. Thank you for
sending love and light to my nose, and shifting it
to perfect health and functionality."*

"Dear Archangel Raphael, I ask that you infuse my ovaries with your emerald green healing light, shining away any blocks or pain and helping them function health-fully in all ways. Thank you for guiding me clearly as to action steps I can take for my health and wellness."

"Dear Archangel Raphael, please bathe my pancreas in your healing energy, helping my digestive and endocrine systems function in Divine and perfect order."

PREGNANCY HEALTH

"Dear Archangel Raphael, I ask that you watch over my baby's growth and health. Please support us fully and clearly, including giving me guidance that I can easily notice and understand so that I know which steps to take to ensure the health and wellness of my baby and myself."

PROSTATE

"Dear Archangel Raphael, thank you for supporting and healing my prostate gland and guiding my actions so that I, too, can ensure its health and functionality."

REPRODUCTIVE SYSTEM

"Dear Archangel Raphael, please send support, guidance, and healing energy to my reproductive system, ensuring that my body is responsive to my desires for pregnancy. I ask that you and the other angels guide me and my partner so that we successfully conceive and give birth to a healthy child."

RESPIRATORY SYSTEM

"Dear Archangel Raphael, I ask that you help me breathe easily, inhaling and exhaling with perfect comfort. Thank you for restoring my respiratory health and for protecting me from pollution, allergens, or other irritants."

RIBS

"Dear Archangel Raphael, thank you for restoring balance to my body and wholeness to my ribs. I am healthy in all ways, in spiritual truth, and I thank you for helping me breathe effortlessly and comfortably."

SHOULDERS

"Dear Archangel Raphael, I now give all burdens to you and God to heal and transmute for me. I am no longer willing to carry negativity or stress, and I ask that you clear and seal my shoulders in your protective and healing green energy."

"Dear Archangel Raphael, thank you for helping me shine God's glorious light through every pore of my skin and to radiate God's natural beauty from head to toe."

"Dear Archangel Raphael, please comfort my mind and help me relax, trust, and let go. Thank you for helping me enjoy a wonderful night's sleep. I now feel safe and loved."

"Dear Archangel Raphael, I now give anything that is upsetting over to you and God for transmuting and healing. I allow myself to accept what is occurring in my life with grace and surrender, knowing that peace creates miraculous healing results. Thank you for infusing my stomach with your healing energy, restoring my digestion to perfect harmony and wellness."

"Dear Archangel Raphael, thank you for bathing my teeth in your healing emerald green energy. Thank you for helping me enjoy healthy teeth."

"Dear Archangel Raphael, I am willing to speak my truth to myself and others with love and wisdom. Thank you for clearing my throat of any fear energies and helping me express myself clearly and healthfully. Thank you for soothing my throat with your green healing energy."

"Dear Archangel Raphael, please help my toe(s) to be healed, healthy, strong, and fully functioning. Please help me stand tall and move forward on the path of my life's purpose. I now release all anger and unforgiveness, in exchange for peace and health."

TONGUE

"Dear Archangel Raphael, I call upon you now. Thank you for releasing fears of speaking up from my past experiences, feelings, or thoughts. Thank you for helping me speak loudly, clearly, and from my heart. Thank you for healing my tongue and restoring it to its Divinely perfect nature."

TONSILS

"Dear Archangel Raphael, please bathe my tonsils in your soothing and healing emerald green light. Thank you for supporting my wellness with clear guidance and healing energy."

TRAVELING

"Dear Archangel Raphael, I ask that you stay with me as my traveling companion along this journey. Thank you for ensuring my safe passage and arrival, with all of my luggage, transportation, food, and lodging needs taken care of in wonderful ways. Thank you for helping my trip to be especially fun, fruitful, and pleasant."

URINARY SYSTEM

"Dear Archangel Raphael, please bathe my urinary system in your healing and balancing green light. I am willing to release all anger and unforgiveness toward myself, others, and circumstances. I now relax my body and let go of anything unhealthful that I have been retaining."

Weight

*"Dear Archangel Raphael, I now give all
thoughts and feelings of burdens and heaviness to
you and God. I am uplifted, and my mind and heart are
light and carefree. Please dissolve any cords of fear
connected to unhealthful foods or beverages, and guide my
appetite and nourishment choices in healthful ways."*

Worry

*"Dear Archangel Raphael, please come to me now and com-
fort my mind and soothe my heart. I am willing to give you
and God all of my cares and worries if you will please assist
me in letting them go. Help me know that I am safe in all
ways. Thank you for shifting my thoughts to peace."*

"*Dear Archangel Raphael, thank you for helping me be flexible. I am now willing to let go of anything unhealthy that I have been clinging to. Thank you for healing my wrists and restoring them to full health and range of motion.*"

ABOUT THE AUTHOR

Doreen Virtue holds B.A., M.A., and Ph.D. degrees in counseling psychology; and is a lifelong clairvoyant who works with the angelic realm. She is the author of the *Healing with the Angels* book and oracle cards; *Archangels & Ascended Masters;* and *Angel Therapy®,* among other works. Her products are available in most languages worldwide.

Doreen has appeared on *Oprah,* CNN, *The View,* and other television and radio programs; and writes regular columns for *Woman's World, New Age Retailer,* and *Spirit & Destiny* magazines. For more information on Doreen and the workshops she presents, please visit: **www .AngelTherapy.com.**

You can listen to Doreen's live weekly radio show, and call her for a reading, by visiting **HayHouseRadio.com®.**

NOTES

NOTES

NOTES

NOTES

NOTES

NOTES

NOTES

NOTES

NOTES

NOTES

NOTES

Hay House Titles of Related Interest

YOU CAN HEAL YOUR LIFE, the movie,
starring Louise L. Hay & Friends
(available as a 1-DVD program and
an expanded 2-DVD set)
Watch the trailer at: **www.LouiseHayMovie.com**

THE SHIFT, the movie,
starring Dr. Wayne W. Dyer
(available as a 1-DVD program and
an expanded 2-DVD set)
Watch the trailer at: **www.DyerMovie.com**

➤➤➤

THE DIVINE NAME:
The Sound That Can Change the World,
by Jonathan Goldman

EXPERIENCE YOUR GOOD NOW!:
Learning to Use Affirmations,
by Louise L. Hay (book-with-CD)

FOR LOVERS OF GOD EVERYWHERE:
Poems of the Christian Mystics,
by Roger Housden

HEALTH, AND THE LAW OF ATTRACTION Cards,
by Esther and Jerry Hicks (The Teachings of Abraham®)

NATURE'S SECRET MESSAGES:
Hidden in Plain Sight, by Elaine Wilkes

THE SHIFT:
Taking Your Life from Ambition to Meaning,
by Dr. Wayne W. Dyer

THE SPONTANEOUS HEALING OF BELIEF:
Shattering the Paradigm of False Limits,
by Gregg Braden

TRAVELING AT THE SPEED OF LOVE,
by Sonia Choquette

All of the above are available at your local
bookstore, or may be ordered by
contacting Hay House (see next page).

We hope you enjoyed this Hay House book.
If you'd like to receive our online catalog featuring
additional information on Hay House books and products,
or if you'd like to find out more about the
Hay Foundation, please contact:

Hay House, Inc., P.O. Box 5100,
Carlsbad, CA 92018-5100

(760) 431-7695 or **(800) 654-5126**
(760) 431-6948 (fax) or **(800) 650-5115 (fax)**
www.hayhouse.com® • **www.hayfoundation.org**

❖❖❖

Published and distributed in Australia by:
Hay House Australia Pty. Ltd., 18/36 Ralph St.,
Alexandria NSW 2015 • *Phone:* 612-9669-4299
Fax: 612-9669-4144 • www.hayhouse.com.au

Published and distributed in the United Kingdom by:
Hay House UK, Ltd., 292B Kensal Rd., London W10 5BE
Phone: 44-20-8962-1230 • *Fax:* 44-20-8962-1239
www.hayhouse.co.uk

*Published and distributed in the Republic of South
Africa by:* Hay House SA (Pty), Ltd., P.O. Box 990,
Witkoppen 2068 • *Phone/Fax:* 27-11-467-8904
info@hayhouse.co.za • www.hayhouse.co.za

Published in India by:
Hay House Publishers India, Muskaan Complex,
Plot No. 3, B-2, Vasant Kunj, New Delhi 110 070
Phone: 91-11-4176-1620 • *Fax:* 91-11-4176-1630
www.hayhouse.co.in

Distributed in Canada by:
Raincoast, 9050 Shaughnessy St., Vancouver, B.C.
V6P 6E5 • *Phone:* (604) 323-7100 • *Fax:* (604) 323-2600
www.raincoast.com

◦◦◦

Take Your Soul on a Vacation

Visit **www.HealYourLife.com**® to regroup, recharge,
and reconnect with your own magnificence.
Featuring blogs, mind-body-spirit news, and life-
changing wisdom from Louise Hay and friends.

Visit **www.HealYourLife.com** today!

Don't miss the latest in books, CDs, movies, and events featuring best-selling author Doreen Virtue

**Angel Therapy®
Oracle Cards**
978-1-4019-1833-0
$15.95 USA · Card Deck

Solomon's Angels
978-1-4019-2324-2
$23.95 USA · 5-CD Set

**The Miracles of
Archangel Michael**
978-1-4019-2205-4
$19.95 USA · Hardcover

Available everywhere books are sold.

See Doreen in a city near you!
Visit **www.angeltherapy.com** for information on upcoming events and lectures.

HAYHOUSE
RADIO))
radio for your soul™
hayhouseradio.com®

HAY
HOUSE
www.hayhouse.com®

HEAL YOUR LIFE♥
www.healyourlife.com®

Mind Your Body,
Mend Your Spirit

Hay House is the ultimate resource for inspirational and health-conscious books, audio programs, movies, events, e-newsletters, member communities, and much more.

Visit **www.hayhouse.com**® today and nourish your soul.

UPLIFTING EVENTS

Join your favorite authors at live events in a city near you or log on to **www.hayhouse.com** to visit with Hay House authors online during live, interactive Web events.

INSPIRATIONAL RADIO

Daily inspiration while you're at work or at home. Enjoy radio programs featuring your favorite authors, streaming live on the Internet 24/7 at **HayHouseRadio.com**®. Tune in and tune up your spirit!

VIP STATUS

Join the Hay House VIP membership program today and enjoy exclusive discounts on books, CDs, calendars, card decks, and more. You'll also receive 10% off all event reservations (excluding cruises). Visit **www.hayhouse.com/wisdom** to join the Hay House Wisdom Community™.

Visit **www.hayhouse.com** and enter priority code 2723
during checkout for special savings!
(One coupon per customer.)

HEAL YOUR LIFE

Take Your Soul on a Vacation

Get your daily dose of inspiration today at **www.HealYourLife.com®**. Brimming with all of the necessary elements to ease your mind and educate your soul, this Website will become the foundation from which you'll start each day. This essential site delivers the latest in mind, body, and spirit news and real-time content from your favorite Hay House authors.

Make It Your Home Page Today!

www.HealYourLife.com®

HAY HOUSE

www.hayhouse.com®